COMPLETE YEAR **K**

Weekly Learning Activities

Thinking Kids™
Carson-Dellosa Publishing LLC
Greensboro, North Carolina

Thinking Kids™
Carson-Dellosa Publishing LLC
P.O. Box 35665
Greensboro, NC 27425 USA

ISBN 978-1-4838-0190-2

Table of Contents

Table of Contents

Table of Contents

Introduction to *Complete Year: Kindergarten*

The *Complete Year* series has been designed by educators to provide an entire school year's worth of practice pages, teaching suggestions, and multi-sensory activities to support your child's learning at home. Handy organizers are included to help students and parents stay on track and to let you see at a glance the important skills for each quarter and each week of the academic year.

A variety of resources are included to help you provide high-quality learning experiences during this important year of your child's development.

Suggested Calendar (Page 7)

Use this recommended timetable to plan learning activities for your child during all 36 weeks of the school year.

A Guide to School Skills for Kindergarten: Basic Skills, Reading and Language Arts, Math, Gross and Fine Motor Skills (Page 8)

Refer to this useful guide for information about what your child will be learning this school year, what to expect from your kindergartner, and how to help your child develop skills in each subject area.

Quarter Introductions (Pages 14, 108, 202, 296)

Four brief introductions outline the skills covered in practice pages for each nine-week grading period of the school year. In addition, they include a variety of ideas for multi-sensory learning activities in each subject area. These active, hands-on projects are fun for parents and children to do together and emphasize real-world applications for school skills.

Weekly Skill Summaries (Example: Page 17)

Thirty-six handy charts precede the practice pages for each week and give a snapshot of the skills covered. In addition, they provide ideas for fun, multi-sensory learning activities for each subject area.

Practice Pages (Example: Page 18)

Nine practice pages are provided each week for a total of over 300 skill-building activities to help your child succeed this year.

Quarter Check-Ups (Pages 107, 201, 295, 389)

Four informal assessment pages allow students to do a quick self-check of the important skills emphasized during the previous nine weeks. Parents can use these pages to see at a glance the skills their children have mastered.

Suggested *Complete Year* Calendar*

First Quarter: Weeks 1–9
(First nine-week grading period of the school year, usually August–October)

Second Quarter: Weeks 10–18
(Second nine-week grading period of the school year, usually October–December)

Third Quarter: Weeks 19–27
(Third nine-week grading period of the school year, usually January–March)

Fourth Quarter: Weeks 28–36
(Fourth nine-week grading period of the school year, usually April–June)

During Each Nine-Week Quarter:

- Read the **Quarter Introduction** to get an overview of the skills and subject areas emphasized. Choose several multi-sensory learning activities you plan to do with your child this quarter.

- Each week, glance at the **Weekly Skill Summary** to see targeted skills. Make a quick plan for the practice pages and multi-sensory learning activities your child will complete.

- Choose **Practice Pages** that emphasize skills your child needs to work on. Each page should take 10 minutes or less to complete.

- Ask your child to check the boxes on the **Quarter Check-Up** to show what skills he or she has mastered. Praise your child's progress and take note of what he or she still needs to work on.

* This calendar provides a schedule for using *Complete Year* during a typical nine-month academic calendar. If your child attends a year-round school or a school with a different schedule, you can easily adapt this calendar by counting the weeks your child attends school and dividing by four.

A Guide to School Skills for Kindergarten

This guide provides background information about the skills and subject areas that are important for success in kindergarten. Tips are provided for helping your child develop in each curricular area.

Complete Year supports skills included in the Kindergarten Common Core State Standards for English Language Arts and Mathematics, which have been adopted by most U.S. states. A complete guide to these standards may be found at www.corestandards.org.

In addition, activities in *Complete Year* support gross motor development and fine motor development, which are essential to a young child's ability to complete schoolwork and regulate behavior.

 Basic Skills

During this first year of formal schooling, your child will be asked to demonstrate an understanding of basic concepts and commands. Activities in this book will help your child work with color names, opposites such as big/small, the concept of same and different, position words, sequencing, and the skill of classifying items into categories. Help your child explore basic skills by providing real-world experiences that encourage thinking and awareness.

- Following Directions
  Give your child short, two- or three-step directions. After he or she successfully completes these, give four-step directions. Following directions requires good listening skills, so make sure you have your child's full attention. Try writing multi-step directions in picture form or create a jingle that incorporates key words from the directions.

- Spatial Concepts
  While the concepts of beside, behind, between, above, and below may seem clear to adults, children need to build their understanding of these ideas. Help by moving toys around and asking your child to describe their positions. Provide further practice by asking your child to move beside or behind something or to describe where he or she is in relation to objects.

- Compare and Contrast
  Help foster your child's ability to observe similarities and differences among objects. Begin with obvious similarities and

differences in color, size, and shape and advance to more subtle similarities and differences in pattern, texture, purpose, etc.

- Classifying
  Organizing objects into categories can be done in many ways. For example, have your child group a set of objects by color, size, pattern, purpose, or other attribute.

- Critical Thinking
  Young children love riddles, jokes, and tongue twisters. Use these word games to develop your child's thinking skills. Critical thinking can be encouraged in many ways. Try asking your child to create a new ending to a familiar story or have him or her be the "teacher" and ask you questions about a story you read together.

 Reading and Language Arts

Reading

In kindergarten, your child is developing reading readiness skills. Reading readiness includes recognizing the letters of the alphabet, knowing the sounds letters make, listening to and following a story that is read aloud, and comprehending the meaning of words.

- Alphabet
  This year, your child will be expected to recognize all 26 letters of the alphabet—both uppercase and lowercase—and to discriminate the letter in the current lesson from letters previously learned.

- Phonics
  An important kindergarten skill is recognizing and discriminating between the different sounds represented by the letters of the alphabet. Consonant sounds (example: /b/ in **boy**) are introduced, reviewed, and covered in a variety of ways. The vowel sounds **short a** (as in **hat**), **short e** (as in **hen**), **short i** (as in **sit**), **short o** (as in **pot**), and **short u** (as in **cup**) are also introduced.

The ability to identify rhyming words shows a child's understanding of the sound patterns of words. Teach your child to listen for and name the rhyming words in a story or poem or to complete a sentence with a word that rhymes. Listening to music is a great way to work with rhyming words.

- Reading Comprehension
Introduce your child to a variety of fiction and nonfiction texts: fairy tales, picture books, poems, folktales, nonfiction books about topics of interest, magazines, diagrams, charts, and tables.

Explore the differences between fantasy and reality. After listening to a text, your child should be able to tell whether the events could really happen or if they are "pretend." Your child will have a better grasp of the concept if you ask him or her to give examples of fantasy (Dogs don't drive cars) or reality (People go to the grocery store).

After reading a fictional story, discuss events that happened at the beginning, middle, and end. Sequencing story events is a good indication of whether or not your child comprehends. Ask your child to look back through the pictures and retell the story. Help develop thinking skills by asking your child to compare and contrast the characters and events from two different stories.

Before reading a nonfiction text, ask your child to listen for certain details or for the answer to a question. This will help your child focus on the information. Follow the reading with some basic questions to check comprehension. Ask questions about vocabulary words, events that came first or last, or causes and effects. If your child is unable to answer your questions from memory, go back and re-read together to find the answers.

- Reading Aloud
Reading aloud to your child will foster his or her desire to learn and read more. As you read to your child, you nurture the following important skills: listening, appreciation of good literature, comprehension, and critical thinking. A list of recommended read-aloud books for kindergartners may be found on page 394.

Language Skills

Language skills are often taught in the context of reading. Your child may be asked to apply knowledge gained from reading to the study of words, sentences, and texts. When reading aloud to your child, take the opportunity to point to individual words, sentences, and punctuation marks on the page and talk about them. This will give your child a deeper understanding of how language works.

- Print Concepts
  In kindergarten, your child will look at text and understand that we read from left to right and from top to bottom. Spaces separate words on a page. Your child will learn to identify parts of a book such as the author name, illustrator name, and cover. He or she will practice reading frequently used words, such as **the** and **it**, by sight.

- Types of Words and Sentences
  This year, your child will learn about types of words and use them to build sentences. For example, he or she will study nouns (or naming words), verbs (or action words), and plurals (or words that name more than one thing). Your child will write sentences that begin with a capital letter and end with a punctuation mark.

- Vocabulary Development
  During kindergarten, your child's vocabulary will grow by leaps and bounds as he or she reads new books, participates in classroom discussions and activities, and interacts with new friends. You may wish to keep a list of new words your child is learning. This year, your child will study opposite words (or antonyms), similar words (or synonyms), and words that have more than one meaning.

Writing

In kindergarten, your child will express ideas by drawing, by dictating to the teacher or another adult, and by writing letters and words on paper. He or she will write to tell stories, share information, and give opinions.

- Handwriting
  Practice pages in this book will help your child print uppercase and lowercase letters correctly. Handwriting is a skill that takes considerable practice for young children. The ability to write by hand is greatly enhanced by the development of fine motor skills (see page 13).

Speaking and Listening

Good speaking and listening skills are essential to school success. Teach your child to maintain good eye contact. By paying careful attention to what is being said, your child will not only learn more but will develop the skill of being a good conversationalist as well. Teach your child that it is impolite to talk with a full mouth, to interrupt, or to finish someone else's sentences. When your child talks to you, model good listening skills. Finally, make sure to provide lots of opportunities in your home for conversation.

Math

Math is an integral part of a young child's world. Everyday experiences such as preparing meals, shopping, and building with blocks provide rich opportunities to explore numbers, shapes, quantities, and patterns. As you go about routines at home with your child, make sure to include discussions about numbers. Let your child see that you use math when you pay bills, make home repairs, or keep a calendar. During the kindergarten year, your child will progress from simple counting tasks to addition and subtraction, working with place value, and more.

- Shapes
  Your child will learn to recognize two-dimensional shapes such as circles, squares, rectangles, triangles, ovals, and rhombuses (or diamonds), and three-dimensional shapes such as cubes, cones, and spheres. Children see shapes in the world around them. Capitalize on this by pointing out different shapes and the way they make up larger objects.

- Counting
  In kindergarten, your child will use numbers to count objects. Counting accurately is a skill that takes some practice for young children. They must learn to associate each item being counted with only one number. They must understand that the last number named represents the total number of items, and that this count is the same regardless of how the items are arranged. Let your child practice by counting real objects. Encourage your child to count up to 20 objects and to count from memory to 100 by ones and by tens.

- Numbers
  Your child will recognize and write numerals **0–20** and use them for counting. He or she will work with ordinal numbers such as **first**, **second**, and **third**.

- Comparing Quantities
  This year, your child will make comparisons in order to tell which has more and which has less. For example, your child will compare two numbers and decide which is greater, compare two groups of objects and decide which has less, or compare two items and decide which is taller.

- Addition and Subtraction
  Your kindergartner will learn to solve addition and subtraction problems within 10, using pictures and objects to represent the problems. He or she will figure out how many more items added to a group will make 10. For numbers **11–19**, your child will think about how many more there are in addition to 10.

 **Gross and Fine Motor Skills**

Developing motor skills is important to your child's physical development. Many people—both adults and children—learn by doing. What may seem like "play" may help your child internalize a concept or skill.

The movement of the large muscle groups is considered gross motor activity. Running, jumping, climbing, throwing a ball, and other activities use the body's large muscles. Your child develops large muscle maturity through active play. Control of the large muscles helps your child move smoothly and control his or her actions.

Many school activities require your child to use the body's small muscle groups to accomplish tasks such as tracing, cutting, writing, folding, and using blocks. These are fine motor skills. Encourage your child to keep working on these skills even though they may be difficult at first. As the small muscles develop, both of you will see improvement in your child's skill level.

First Quarter Introduction

The first weeks of kindergarten are exciting for your child and for the whole family. Be positive and encouraging as your child begins this new adventure. During the first quarter of the new school year, take advantage of your child's enthusiasm for learning. This is a great time to take stock of what your child already knows well and to tackle some new challenges.

First Quarter Skills

Practice pages in this book for Weeks 1–9 will help your child improve the following skills.

Basic Skills
- Identify and review colors red, yellow, blue, green, orange, purple, black, brown, and pink
- Understand the concept of same/different

Reading and Language Arts
- Recognize uppercase and lowercase letters **Aa-Rr**
- Write uppercase and lowercase letters **Aa-Rr**

Math
- Identify and draw these shapes: circle, square, triangle, rectangle, oval, rhombus
- Work with shape and picture patterns

Multi-Sensory Learning Activities

Try these fun activities for enhancing your child's learning and development during the first quarter of the school year. Be sure to choose activities that include speaking, listening, touching, and active movement.

 Basic Skills

Drop food coloring into glasses of water. Ask your child to name each color. After making red, yellow, and blue (the primary colors), have your child experiment to see how to make orange, purple, and green (the secondary colors).

Take a walk around the block. Give directions such as "stop if you see red" or "run if you see yellow."

Provide an assortment of buttons or small toys. Encourage your child to choose two items and talk about how they are the same and different. Then, encourage your child to sort all the objects by color, size, shape, etc.

 Reading and Language Arts

Sing the alphabet song together. Have your child jump up, clap, or do another motion when a letter is sung that is included in his or her first name.

Spin a top. Before it stops, challenge your child to say as many words as he or she can that begin with **b**, **d**, **f**, **g**, **h**, **j**, **l**, **m**, **n**, **p**, or **r**.

Choose a letter of the alphabet. Go on a scavenger hunt in your home to find that letter in books, on food packages, on junk mail, etc.

Cut out a giant construction paper letter. Have your child cut pictures out of magazines that begin with that letter and glue them on.

When reading together, play "I Spy a Word." Give clues to one word on the page, telling how many letters it contains, what letter it begins or ends with, etc. Can your child find and point to the word?

 **Math**

Provide shape stencils or make some from cardstock. Let your child trace around each shape, holding the stencil securely with the non-writing hand. Can your child describe and name each shape?

Use your arms to make large circles in the air while reciting this rhyme: Here is a circle, all smooth and round/Where are the sides?/There are none to be found!

Cut sponges into shapes. Allow your child to dip them in finger paint and use as stamps to create designs or pictures.

Find something that is square (such as a pizza box) and something that is rectangular (such as a book). Let your child use a tape measure to measure all four sides of each object. How are squares and rectangles different?

Set out a variety of coins. Let your child use them to make simple patterns such as penny, nickel, penny, nickel….

First Quarter Introduction, cont.

 ### Fine Motor Skills

Let your child glue toothpicks onto construction paper to make these shapes: square, rectangle, triangle, rhombus.

Make paper dolls to represent your family. Fold a sheet of paper accordion-style, then cut out the shape of a person, being careful to keep the folded side intact. Use crayons to add features to the dolls.

Make vanilla instant pudding. Divide it into bowls and let your child help use food coloring to tint the pudding in each bowl a different color. Let your child finger paint with the pudding colors on a cookie tray.

 ### Gross Motor Skills

Name a letter and think of an action that begins with that letter. Have your child perform the action while chanting the letter name and words that begin with it. For example, bounce while saying "B, B, B, bicycles, babies, butterflies!"

Plan an obstacle course for your child full of commands that begin with one letter. For the letter **c**, you might ask your child to carry a cup across the room, crawl under a table, and crunch a cracker.

 ### Seasonal Fun

Read *Autumn: An Alphabet Acrostic* by Steven Schnur. Help your child write his or her own acrostic poem about autumn.

Read *The Tiny Seed* by Eric Carle. Go on a hike and collect pinecones, maple wings (helicopters), acorns, and thistles. Talk about how seeds travel. Some are winged to help them flutter down. Others are sticky or prickly to attach to people and animals. Others are plumed (dandelions) so the wind carries them. Open the protective cases you found to see the actual seeds inside.

Use leaves your child collects to make leaf rubbings. Put a thin sheet of white paper over the underside of each leaf and gently rub the paper with the side of a crayon.

Week 1 Skills

Subject	Skill	Multi-Sensory Learning Activities
Reading and Language Arts	Recognize and write the letters **A** and **a**.	• Complete Practice Pages 18 and 19. • Drag the wheels of a toy airplane through finger paint. Roll it on drawing paper to write **A** and **a**. • Cut two apple shapes from construction paper. Staple them halfway together to form a pocket. Fill the pocket with pictures of things that have the **short a** sound.
	Recognize and write the letters **B** and **b**.	• Complete Practice Pages 20 and 21. • Think of things to eat that begin with the **b** sound. Then, have a snack of bananas or bagels. • Glue dried beans on construction paper in the shape of **B** and **b**.
Basic Skills	Work with the colors red, yellow, blue, green, and orange.	• Complete Practice Pages 22–26. • Make a little book with a riddle about a color on each page. Here is one: What is orange and sounds like a parrot? A carrot!
Bonus: Math		• Practice counting every day. Count the number of steps you climb, the number of toys in a basket, or the number of forks in a drawer.
Bonus: Fine Motor Skills		• Make "ants on a log" by spreading cream cheese on a celery stalk and adding raisins. Show how to use the index finger and thumb together to pick up each raisin.

Letter Aa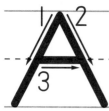

UPPERCASE

lowercase

These pictures begin with the letter **A**, **a**. Color the pictures.

Letter Aa

Color the **A**s red. Color the **a**s green. Color the other letters yellow.

Letter Bb

UPPERCASE

B

lowercase

b

These pictures begin with the letter **B**, **b**. Color the pictures.

Letter Bb

Color to find the hidden picture. Color the spaces with **B** blue. Color the spaces with **b** yellow. Color the other spaces with a color you like.

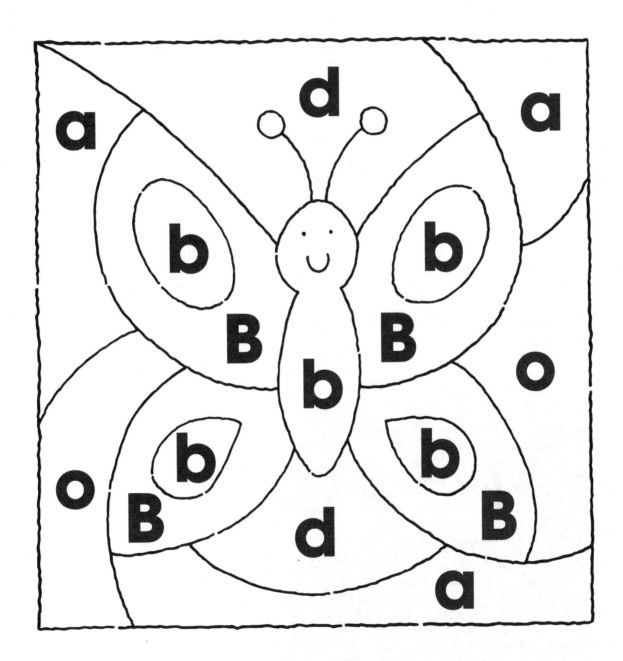

What did you find? _____

Red

Color each picture red. Then, draw a picture of something else red.

Color each picture yellow. Then, draw a picture of something else yellow.

Blue

Circle the blue picture in each row.

Green

Color each picture green. Then, draw a picture of something else green.

Orange

Circle the orange picture in each row.

Week 2 Skills

Subject	Skill	Multi-Sensory Learning Activities
Reading and Language Arts	Recognize and write the letters **C** and **c**.	• Complete Practice Pages 28 and 29. • Play "I Spy a **C** Word." Give clues such as "It is an animal with fur. It chases mice. What is it? A cat!" Let your child give you clues to **C** words, too. • Show how a dry piece of elbow macaroni resembles the letter **c**. Draw a large **c** outline on construction paper. Let your child glue on macaroni pieces to fill the letter shape.
	Recognize and write the letters **D** and **d**.	• Complete Practice Pages 30 and 31. • In a shallow container full of sand, hide small items including a few that begin with **d** such as a die, a dime, or a doll. Let your child dig for **d** words! • Use refrigerated dough to make doughnuts. Show your child how to shape the dough into **D** and **d** shapes. Fry the dough in hot oil while your child stands back. Coat the doughnuts in cinnamon and sugar and enjoy!
Basic Skills	Work with the colors purple, black, and brown. Review all colors.	• Complete Practice Pages 32–35. • Blow up balloons of different colors. Help your child use a permanent marker to label each balloon with a color word.
Bonus: Math		• Give your child a bag and a "shopping" list that uses only numbers and pictures. Ask him or her to put the appropriate number of each item into the bag.
Bonus: Gross Motor Skills		• Play charades. Pretend to be a character or creature that begins with **d** such as a dragon, dwarf, dog, or duck. Can your child guess who you are? Take turns.

Letter Cc

UPPERCASE

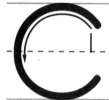

lowercase

These pictures begin with the letter **C**, **c**. Color the pictures.

Letter Cc

Look at the patterns on the cats' sweaters. Draw a line between the cats with matching **Cc** patterns on their sweaters.

Letter Dd

UPPERCASE

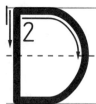

lowercase

These pictures begin with the letter **D**, **d**. Color the pictures.

Letter Dd

Help the dolphin jump through the rings. Color the rings that have the letter **D** or **d** in them.

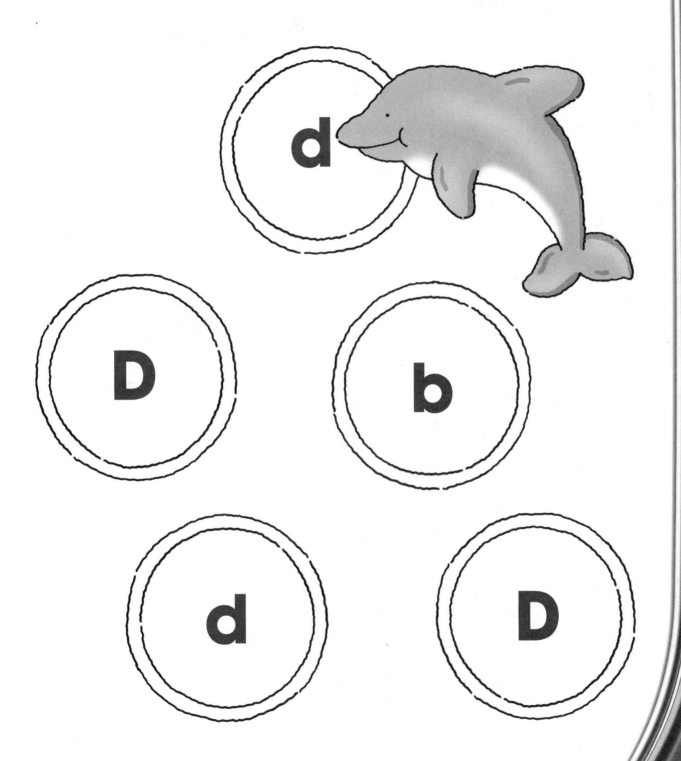

Purple

Color each picture purple. Then, draw a picture of something else purple.

Black

Circle the black picture in each row.

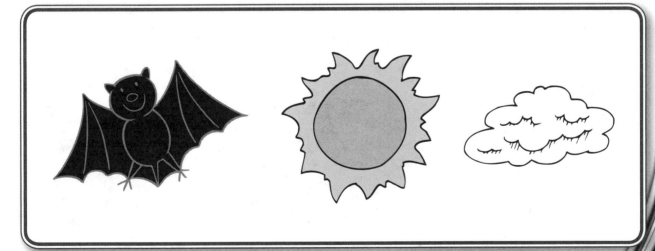

Brown

Circle the brown picture in each row.

Review Colors

Cut out the shapes below and glue them in the correct color box.

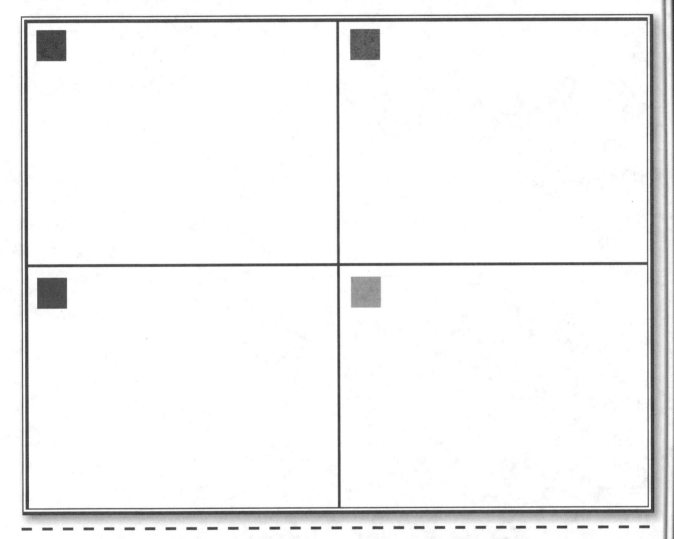

Week 3 Skills

Subject	Skill	Multi-Sensory Learning Activities
Reading and Language Arts	Recognize and write the letters **E** and **e**.	• Complete Practice Pages 38 and 39. • Have your child use rope licorice to form **E** and **e**. • Play a game with plastic eggs. Put magnetic letters in one set and pictures of things that begin with those letters in another set. Can your child match the eggs?
	Recognize and write the letters **F** and **f**.	• Complete Practice Pages 40–42. • Read *One Fish, Two Fish, Red Fish, Blue Fish* by Dr. Seuss. Challenge your child to read the number and color words and to point to the letter **F** or **f** on each page. • Take turns with your child drawing things that begin with **f** such as a fish, face, fox, or finger. How many can you think of?
Basic Skills	Review colors.	• Complete Practice Pages 43–46. • Teach your child the mnemonic **Roy G. Biv** to help remember the colors of the rainbow: red, orange, yellow, green, blue, indigo, violet. Ask your child to draw a rainbow!
Bonus: Math		• Provide fish-shaped crackers for your child to count. Can he or she put some in one bowl and a greater number in another bowl?
Bonus: Gross Motor Skills		• Hide several feathers from the craft store in different areas of your home. Can your child find them? Tell your child when he or she is "hot" or "cold."

Letter Ee

UPPERCASE

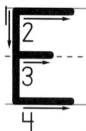

lowercase

These pictures begin with the letter **E**, **e**. Color the pictures.

Letter Ee

Help the baby elephant get to its mother. Color the footprints with **E** or **e** on them.

Letter Ff

UPPERCASE

lowercase

These pictures begin with the letter **F**, **f**. Color the pictures.

Letter Ff

Color the fish in the fish bowl. Color the **F** fish orange. Color the **f** fish green. Color the other fish with a color you like.

Review Aa–Ff

Circle the letters in each row that match the first letter.

A	B	A	D	B
b	d	b	a	d
C	O	F	E	C
d	h	a	b	d
E	E	F	E	A
f	t	f	l	o

Colors

Circle the orange picture in each row.

Colors

Circle the pink picture in each row.

Colors

Circle the purple picture in each row.

Colors

Circle the brown picture in each row.

Week 4 Skills

Subject	Skill	Multi-Sensory Learning Activities
Reading and Language Arts	Recognize and write the letters **G** and **g**.	• Complete Practice Pages 48 and 49. • Provide two long "gold" necklaces. Can your child use them to make **G** and **g** shapes? • Give your child a few dollars to spend at a discount store. Can he or she buy you a gift that begins with **g**? Buy your child a **g** gift, too.
	Recognize and write the letters **H** and **h**.	• Complete Practice Pages 50–52. • Collect pictures of things that begin with **h** such as a horse, a hat, or a house. Punch a hole in each picture and use yarn to suspend it from a hanger to make a mobile. • Read *Old Hat, New Hat* by Stan and Jan Berenstain. Can your child find the letter **H** or **h** on each page?
Math	Recognize and draw circles.	• Complete Practice Pages 53 and 54. • Make up circle riddles. For example, say, "I am a circle on the wall. I have hands and numbers. What am I? A clock!"
	Recognize and draw squares.	• Complete Practice Pages 55 and 56. • Challenge your child to draw a robot, train, house, or other object using only squares. • Cut squares and circles from construction paper. Have your child glue them together to make a truck or another object.
Bonus: Fine Motor Skills		• Shop for square origami paper. Find directions for using it to make simple shapes such as boats or swans.

Letter Gg

UPPERCASE

lowercase

These pictures begin with the letter **G**, **g**. Color the pictures.

Letter Gg

Circle the letter **G** or **g** in each box.

Letter Hh

UPPERCASE

lowercase

These pictures begin with the letter **H**, **h**. Color the pictures.

COMPLETE YEAR KINDERGARTEN

Letter Hh

Color to find the hidden picture. Color the spaces with **H** blue. Color the spaces with **h** brown.

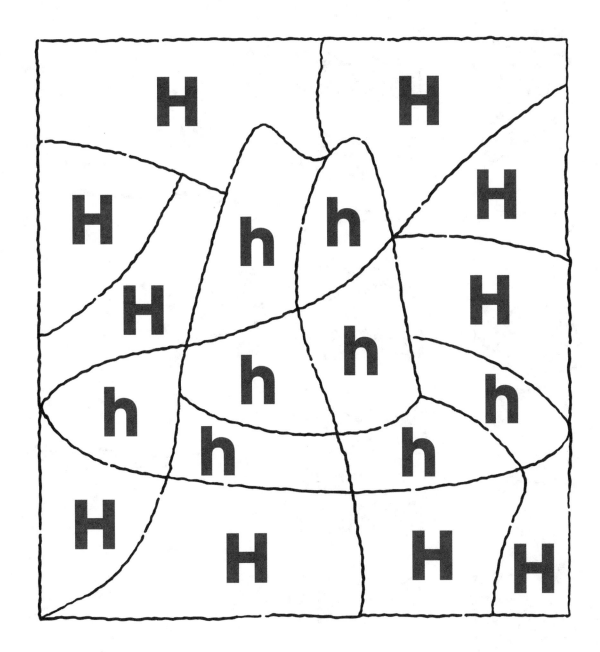

What did you find? _____

Review Ff–Hh

Draw a line from each uppercase letter to its matching lowercase letter.

Circles

Trace the circle below. Draw a circle. Then, draw a line under the circle in each row.

Circles

Draw an **X** on the pictures that have the shape of a circle.

Squares

Trace the square below. Draw a square. Then, draw a line under the square in each row.

Squares

Draw an **X** on the pictures that have the shape of a square.

Week 5 Skills

Subject	Skill	Multi-Sensory Learning Activities
Reading and Language Arts	Recognize and write the letters **I** and **i**.	• Complete Practice Pages 58 and 59. • Show your child the liquid ink inside a pen. Help him or her write **I** and **i** with ink.
	Recognize and write the letters **J** and **j**.	• Complete Practice Pages 60–62. • Can your child shape a jump rope to make the letters **J** and **j**? • Sing this song to the tune of "Row, Row Your Boat": Jump, jump, jump for joy/ Jump for letter **J**/Jump, jump, jump for joy/For **J**s we say Hooray!
Math	Recognize and draw triangles.	• Complete Practice Pages 63 and 64. • Go on a "Triangle Hunt" around your home. Make a list of things shaped like triangles. • Cut several circles, squares, and triangles from cardboard and place them in a bag. Name one shape. Can your child reach in without looking and find it?
	Recognize and draw rectangles.	• Complete Practice Pages 65 and 66. • Look through a picture book with your child. How many things can you find with a rectangle shape? • Find a framed picture, book, or other item in your home. Is it a rectangle or a square? Measure the sides to find out.
Bonus: Basic Skills		• Fill a large sheet of drawing paper with shape outlines. Then, give your child directions to follow. For example, say, "Color the small triangle blue. Make a smiley face inside the circle at the top of the page."

Letter Ii

UPPERCASE

lowercase

These pictures begin with the letter **I**, **i**. Color the pictures.

Letter Ii

Help the inchworm get to the flower. Circle the letters
I and **i**.

Letter Jj

UPPERCASE

lowercase

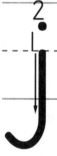

These pictures begin with the letter **J**, **j**. Color the pictures.

COMPLETE YEAR KINDERGARTEN

Letter Jj

Jim has a ticket for a ride. Color to find the hidden picture. Color the spaces with **J** or **j** blue. Color the other spaces gray.

What will Jim ride in? _____

Review A–J

Help the walrus get back to the sea by following the letters in ABC order.

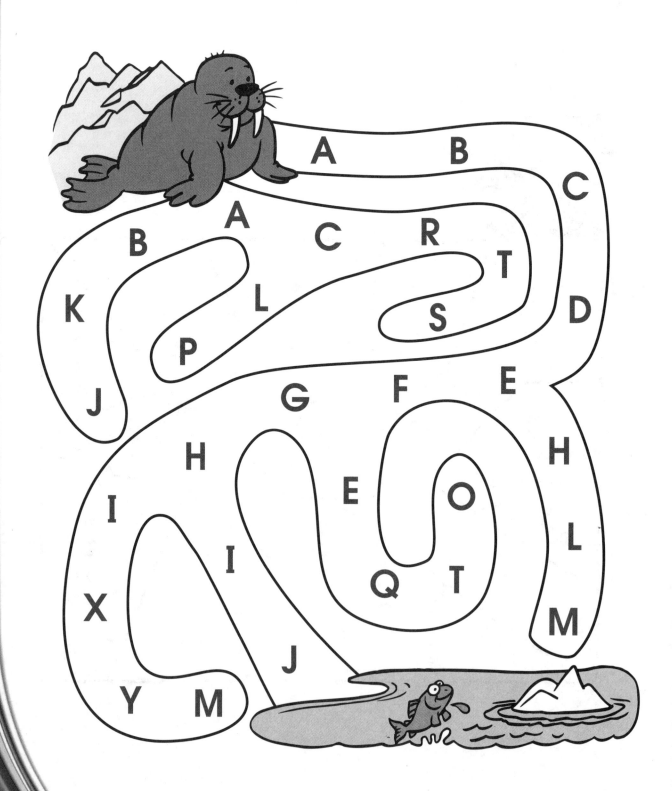

COMPLETE YEAR KINDERGARTEN

Triangles

Trace the triangle below. Draw a triangle. Then, draw a line under the triangle in each row.

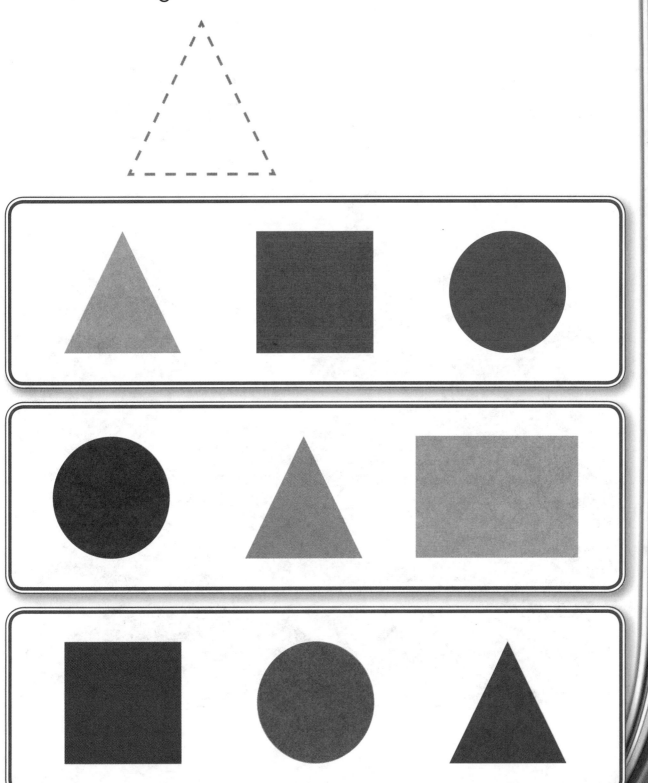

Triangles

Draw an **X** on the pictures that have the shape of a triangle.

Rectangles

Trace the rectangle below. Draw a rectangle. Then, draw a line under the rectangle in each row.

Rectangles

Draw an **X** on the pictures that have the shape of a rectangle.

Week 6 Skills

Subject	Skill	Multi-Sensory Learning Activities
Reading and Language Arts	Recognize and write the letters **K** and **k**.	• Complete Practice Pages 68 and 69. • Make a construction paper crown your child can wear to be the "King of **K**." Encourage your child to decorate the crown with pictures of things that begin with **k** such as keys, kites, and kangaroos. • Use masking tape to form a giant **k** on the floor or draw one outside with sidewalk chalk. Have your child hop along the letter like a kangaroo.
	Recognize and write the letters **L** and **l**.	• Complete Practice Pages 70–72. • Challenge your child to form **l** and **L** shapes with his or her body. • Draw a ladder on a large sheet of paper. Can your child name words that begin with **l**? Write one word on each ladder rung.
Math	Recognize and draw ovals.	• Complete Practice Pages 73 and 74. • Can your child use a rubber band to form a circle? Can he or she "squash" it to make an oval shape? • Draw an oval. Ask your child to add to the drawing to make the oval into a rabbit ear, a submarine, or something else. What can you make from a shape your child draws?
	Recognize and draw rhombuses.	• Complete Practice Pages 75 and 76. • Cut two triangles from paper. Can your child put them together to make a rhombus? Talk about the difference between a rhombus and a square.
Bonus: Fine Motor Skills		• Cut lengths of yarn for you and your child. Make different shapes with your yarn. Have your child imitate the shapes you make.

Letter Kk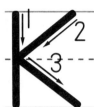

UPPERCASE

lowercase

These pictures begin with the letter **K**, **k**. Color the pictures.

Letter Kk

Look at the letters on each key and lock. Draw a line between the keys and locks with matching letters.

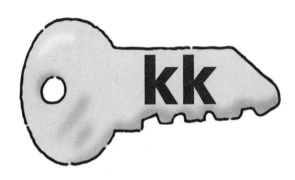

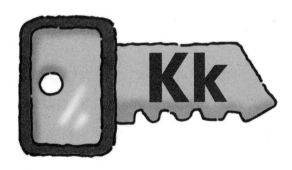

Letter Ll

UPPERCASE

lowercase

These pictures begin with the letter **L**, **l**. Color the pictures.

Letter Ll

Look at the letters. Color the objects with the letter **L** or **l**.

Review Jj–Ll

Circle the letters in each row that match the first letter.

J	**J**	**U**	**L**	**J**
j	**g**	**j**	**q**	**i**
K	**N**	**F**	**H**	**K**
k	**l**	**h**	**k**	**b**
L	**J**	**I**	**L**	**U**
l	**t**	**i**	**l**	**i**

COMPLETE YEAR KINDERGARTEN

Ovals

Trace the oval below. Draw an oval. Then, draw a line under the oval in each row.

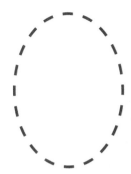

Ovals

Draw an **X** on the pictures that have the shape of an oval.

Rhombuses

Trace the rhombus below. Draw a rhombus. Then, draw a line under the rhombus in each row.

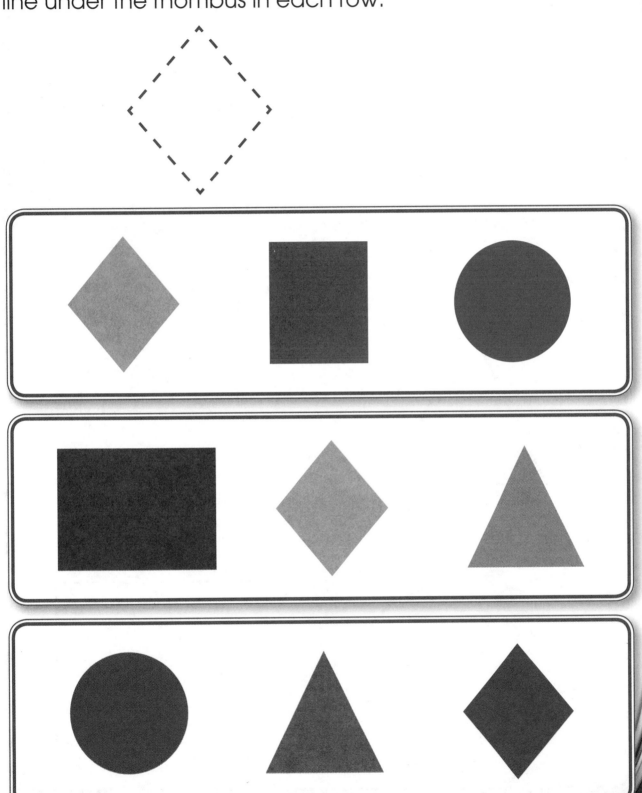

Rhombuses

Color the rhombuses.

Week 7 Skills

Subject	Skill	Multi-Sensory Learning Activities
Reading and Language Arts	Recognize and write the letters **M** and **m**.	• Complete Practice Pages 78 and 79. • Use glue on colored paper to form **M** and **m**. Cover the letters with miniature marshmallows. • Ask your child to place pictures of things that begin with **m** inside separate envelopes and then deliver the "mail" to your home's mailbox. Open the mail together, writing an **m** word on each envelope to match the picture.
	Recognize and write the letters **N** and **n**.	• Complete Practice Pages 80 and 81. • Give your child a sheet from a newspaper. Ask him or her to circle each **N** or **n** found on the page. • Give your child one minute. How many things can he or she find in your home that begin with **n**?
Basic Skills	Understand the concept of same/different.	• Complete Practice Pages 83–86. • Set out two similar objects such as a dish towel and a hot pad. Have your child describe the similarities and differences between them. • Provide a handful of different coins. Let your child sort them into piles, noting their similarities and differences.
Bonus: Math		• Have a snack of square crackers and round cookies. Invite your child to make a pattern such as circle, circle, square, circle, circle….

Letter Mm

UPPERCASE

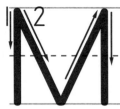

lowercase

These pictures begin with the letter **M**, **m**. Color the pictures.

Letter Mm

Color to find the hidden picture. Color the spaces with **M** gray. Color the spaces with **m** yellow. Color the other spaces with a color you like.

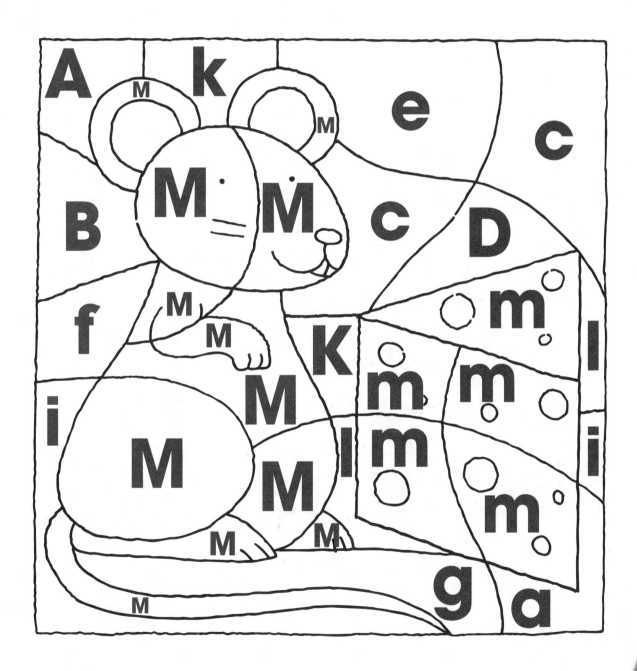

What did you find? _____

Letter Nn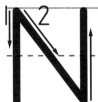

UPPERCASE

lowercase

These pictures begin with the letter **N**, **n**. Color the pictures.

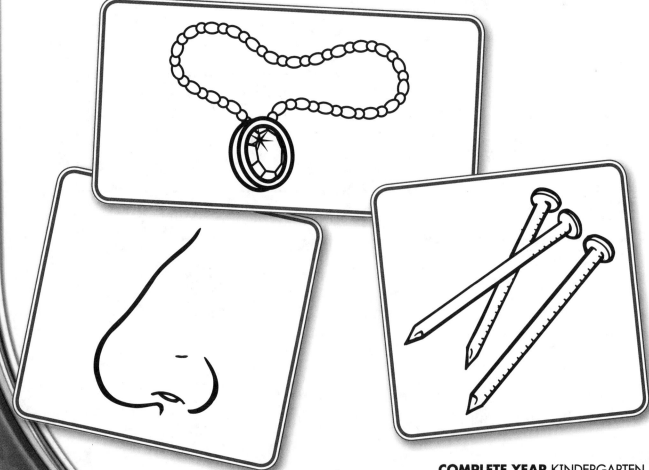

Letter Nn

Cut out the eggs with **N** or **n** on them. Then, glue them in the nest below.

Same

Look at the shapes in each row. Color the shape that is the same as the first shape in each row.

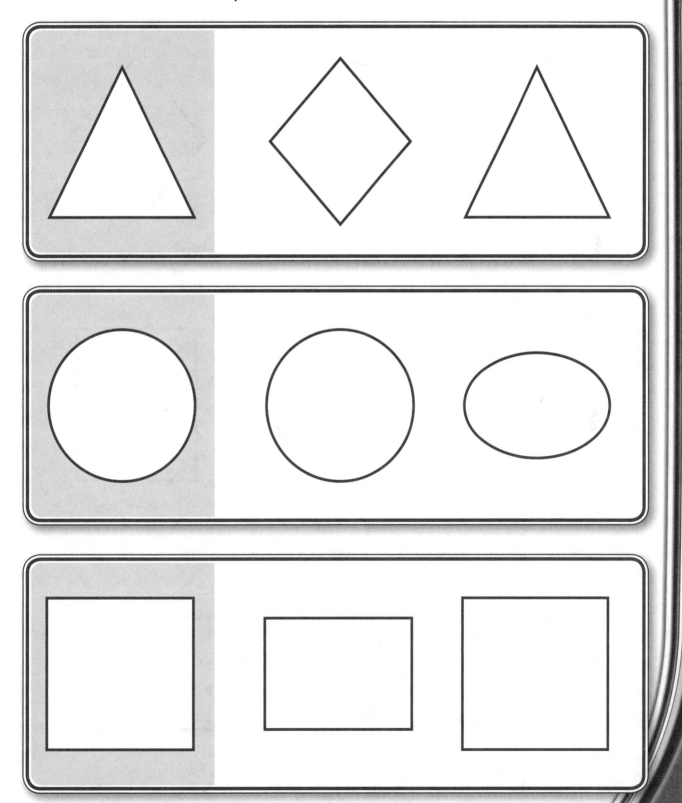

Same

Look at the shapes in each row. Color the shape that is the same as the first shape in each row.

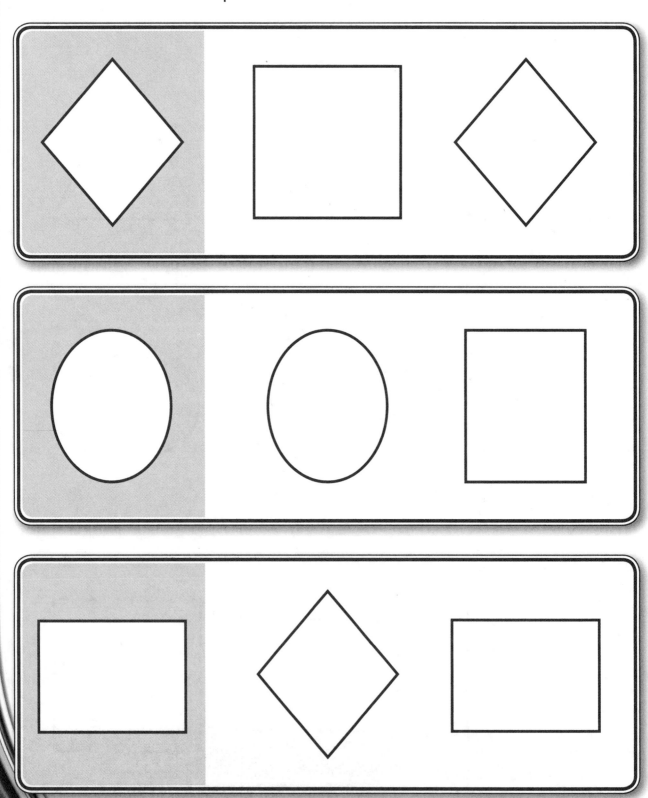

Different

Color the shape in each row that is different.

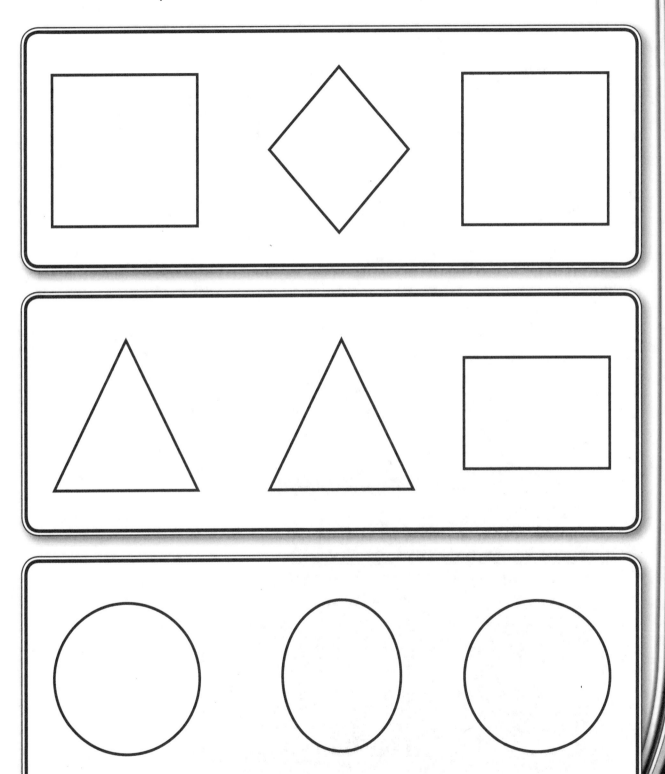

Different

Color the shape in each row that is different.

Week 8 Skills

Subject	Skill	Multi-Sensory Learning Activities
Reading and Language Arts	Recognize and write the letters **O** and **o**.	• Complete Practice Pages 88 and 89. • Play with magnetic letters. Have your child put **o** between consonants to make **pot**, **mop**, and **sob**. Say the words together, emphasizing the **short o** sound. • Cut an onion in half. Let your child separate the rings to make **O** and **o** shapes.
	Recognize and write the letters **P** and **p**.	• Complete Practice Pages 90 and 91. • Let your child mix pancake batter. Pour the batter into the pan in the shapes of **P** and **p**. Enjoy eating the **Pp** pancakes! • Read the poem "Ride a Purple Pelican" by Jack Prelutsky, found in the book of the same name. Point to each **P** and **p** you find.
Math	Work with shape patterns.	• Complete Practice Pages 93–96. • Cut 10 or more shapes from paper of different colors. Let your child use them to make patterns. Can you choose the next shape for the pattern your child made? Make patterns for your child to solve, too.
Bonus: Basic Skills		• Have your child tell you the order of steps needed to load the dishwasher, feed a pet, or do a similar activity.
Bonus: Fine Motor Skills		• Invite one of your child's friends over to do a project together such as working a jigsaw puzzle or building a tower of sugar cubes.

Letter Oo

UPPERCASE

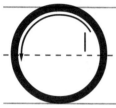

lowercase

These pictures begin with the letter **O**, **o**. Color the pictures.

Letter Oo

What did the octopus see on the ocean floor? Color the spaces with **O** or **o** blue. Color the other spaces brown.

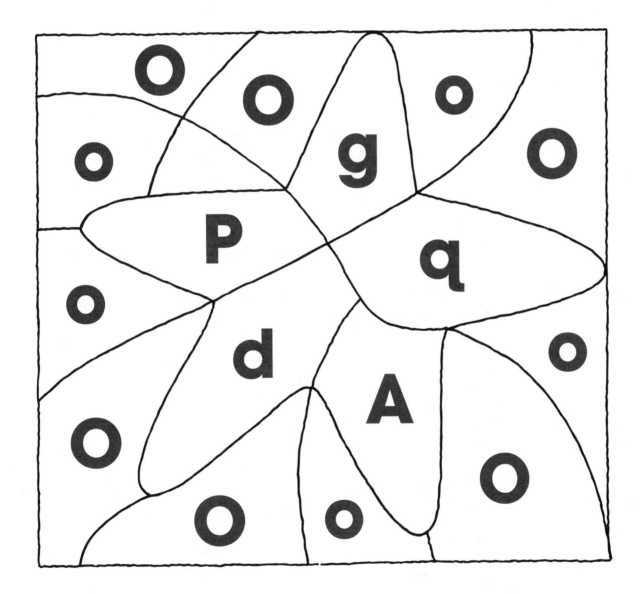

What did the octopus see? _____

Letter Pp

UPPERCASE

lowercase

These pictures begin with the letter **P**, **p**. Color the pictures.

Letter Pp

Cut out the party hats with **P** or **p**. Glue them on the children's heads.

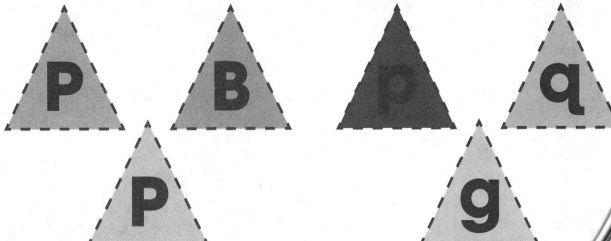

Shape Patterns

Circle the shape that comes next in each pattern.

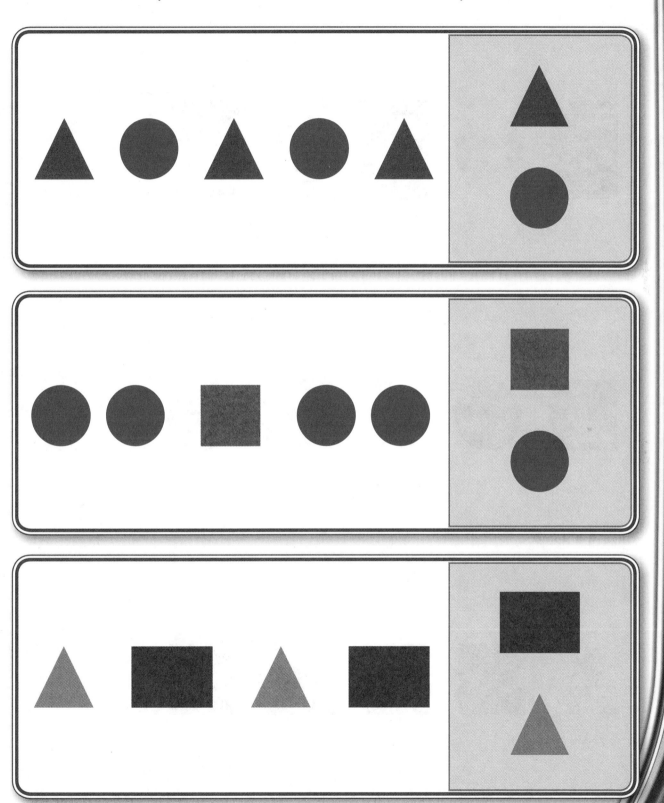

Shape Patterns

Draw and color the shape that comes next in each pattern.

Shape Patterns

Draw and color the shape that comes next in each pattern.

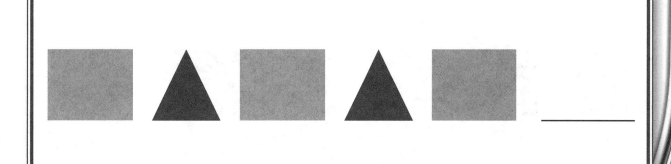

Shape Patterns

Draw the shape that comes next in each pattern.

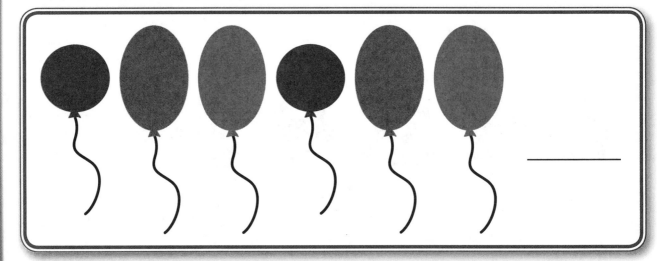

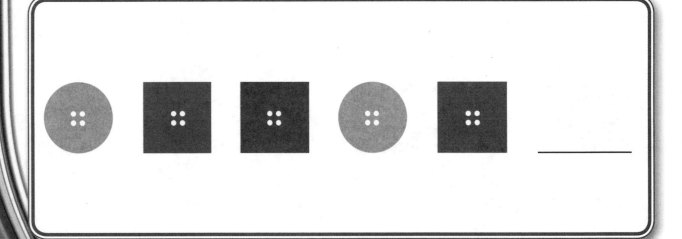

COMPLETE YEAR KINDERGARTEN

Week 9 Skills

Subject	Skill	Multi-Sensory Learning Activities
Reading and Language Arts	Recognize and write the letters **Q** and **q**.	• Complete Practice Pages 98 and 99. • Cut small squares from scrap fabric. Have your child glue them to paper to make a quilt. He or she can write **Q** and **q** on the squares with a fabric marker. • Compare the sounds made by the letters **k** and **q**, noticing the different position of the lips when making each sound. Then, teach your child this rhyme: Q, Q, quiet Q/Q, Q, I love you!
	Recognize and write the letters **R** and **r**.	• Complete Practice Pages 100 and 101. • Collect small rocks. Arrange them on the sidewalk in the shape of **R** and **r**. Have your child trace the letters lightly, beginning at the top. • Have your child dictate the story "Little Red Riding Hood" while you write his or her words. Then, read the story together, pointing to the letters **R** and **r** when they appear in the text.
Math	Work with picture patterns.	• Complete Practice Pages 103–105. • Print a number of small pictures from the Internet that represent your child's interests, such as trucks or fairies. Encourage your child to arrange the pictures to form patterns. Can you guess what the next picture in your child's pattern should be?
Bonus: Gross Motor Skills		• Make up a pattern of actions, such as clap, clap, jump, snap, clap, clap, jump…. Can your child follow your pattern? Have your child make an action pattern for you, too.

Letter Qq

UPPERCASE

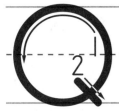

lowercase

These pictures begin with the letter **Q**, **q**. Color the pictures.

Letter Qq

Color the quilt. Color the squares with **Q** green. Color the squares with **q** pink.

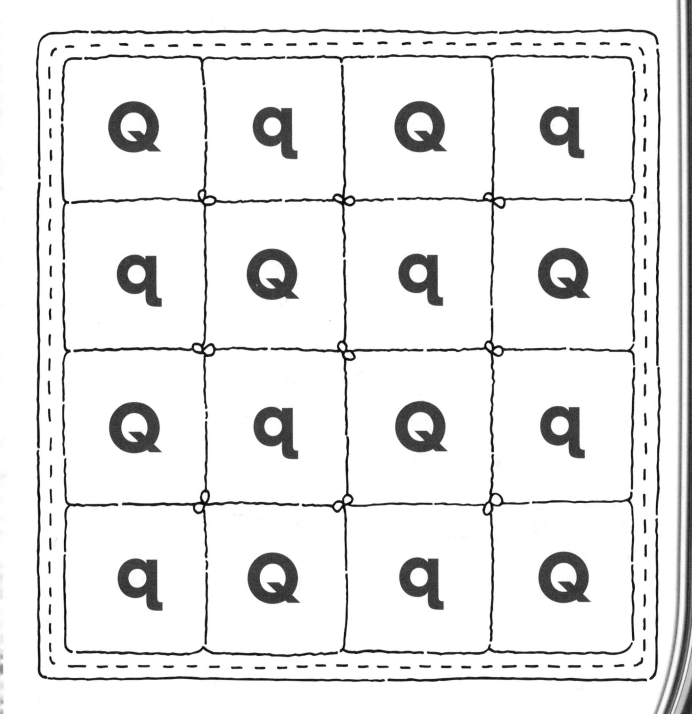

Letter Rr

UPPERCASE

lowercase

These pictures begin with the letter **R**, **r**. Color the pictures.

Letter Rr

Help finish the umbrella. Cut out the pieces with **R** or **r** on them. Then, glue them in the correct places.

Patterns

Complete the picture patterns. At the end of the row, draw the picture that comes next.

Patterns

Complete the picture patterns. Draw what is missing on the last picture in each row.

Patterns

Complete the picture patterns. Cut out the pictures at the bottom of the page. At the end of that row, glue the picture that comes next.

First Quarter Check-Up

Basic Skills

❑ I know these colors: red, yellow, blue, green, orange, purple, black, and brown.

❑ I can point out which things are the same.

❑ I can point out which things are different.

Reading and Language Arts

❑ I recognize these uppercase letters: **A, B, C, D, E, F, G, H, I, J, K, L, M, N, O, P, Q, R.**

❑ I recognize these lowercase letters: **a, b, c, d, e, f, g, h, i, j, k, l, m, n, o, p, q, r.**

❑ I can write these uppercase letters: **A, B, C, D, E, F, G, H, I, J, K, L, M, N, O, P, Q, R.**

❑ I can write these lowercase letters: **a, b, c, d, e, f, g, h, i, j, k, l, m, n, o, p, q, r.**

Math

❑ I recognize circles and squares.

❑ I recognize triangles and rectangles.

❑ I recognize ovals and rhombuses.

❑ I can complete patterns.

Final Project

Use a large package of pipe cleaners from the craft store to make a collection of 26 lowercase letters. Trace each letter with your finger, starting at the top. Use the letters to spell your name, color words, and other words you know.

Use more pipe cleaners to make shapes. Can you make a pattern with the shapes?

Second Quarter Introduction

During the second quarter of the school year, many children are settled into routines at home and at school. Make sure your family's routines include time for playing, eating and talking together, and reading aloud. Supporting your child's learning and development will build his or her confidence in all areas.

Second Quarter Skills

Practice pages in this book for Weeks 10–18 will help your child improve the following skills.

Basic Skills
- Understand opposites such as long/short and big/small
- Understand position words such as **above**, **below**, and **between**

Reading and Language Arts
- Recognize uppercase and lowercase letters **Ss–Zz**
- Write uppercase and lowercase letters **Ss–Zz**
- Match uppercase and lowercase letters
- Review letters **Aa–Zz**
- Identify sounds made by the consonant letters **b, c, d, f, g, h, j, k, l, m, n, p, q, r, s, t, v, w,** and **x**

Math
- Distinguish between two-dimensional and three-dimensional shapes
- Build larger shapes from smaller shapes
- Recognize numbers **0–7**
- Write numbers **0–7**
- Count 0–7 objects

Multi-Sensory Learning Activities

Try these fun activities for enhancing your child's learning and development during the second quarter of the school year. Be sure to choose activities that include speaking, listening, touching, and active movement.

 Basic Skills

Read *Exactly the Opposite* by Tana Hoban. Invite your child to describe the photograph on each page.

Write directions on slips of paper and place them in a bowl. Have your child draw one and do what it says. Include directions such as "Place a penny between two spoons" or "Put a doll on top of the table." Make sure to include these position words in your directions: **top**, **bottom**, **above**, **below**, **near**, **far**, **between**, **beside**, **high**, **low**, **over**, **under**.

 Reading and Language Arts

Give your child a page from a newspaper or magazine. Then, give directions such as these: Draw a circle around each **t** you find. Draw a square around each **u**. Underline each **S**. Cross out each **Y**.

Say or write sentences like the ones below and ask your child to complete each with a word that has the same beginning letter as the other words in the sentence.

Brandon believes _____.   Carly collects _____.

Tigers tickle_____.   She sells _____.

Write letters on self-sticking notes. In two minutes, can your child place each note on something in your home that begins with that letter?

While traveling in the car, look for a sign with **A** or **a** on it. Then, challenge your child to find a sign with **B** or **b**. Take turns. See if you can find all the letters to **Zz**.

2 8 4
9 6 **Math**

Take a walk outside or through a shopping mall. See if you can spot three-dimensional objects shaped like cones, cubes, and spheres.

Work with a group of pencils, twigs, stacks of interlocking blocks, or lengths of yarn. Ask your child to count the items in the group. Can your child arrange the items from shortest to longest? From longest to shortest?

Dictate a picture for your child to draw. Include specific numbers of objects. For example, ask your child to draw three pumpkins on a fence, two children standing next to the fence, and five leaves floating down.

Ask your child to write numbers **0–7** down the left edge of a large sheet of drawing paper. Then, in a row beside each number, have your child glue that many pieces of dry cereal.

Second Quarter Introduction, cont.

Write numbers **0-7** on one set of index cards. Write number words **zero-seven** on a second set of cards. On a third set of cards, affix 0 stickers, 1 sticker, 2 stickers…7 stickers. Mix up all the cards. Can your child match them?

 Fine Motor Skills

Spray shaving cream onto a cookie sheet. Let your child use the index finger of his or her writing hand to form uppercase and lowercase letters and numbers **0-7** in the cream.

Help your child cut seven umbrella shapes from construction paper. Decorate the umbrellas and write a number **1-7** on each. Bend pipe cleaners in the shape of handles and tape one to the back of each umbrella. Then, help your child cut out a number of small raindrop shapes from blue paper and punch a hole in each. Can your child choose an umbrella and thread the matching number of raindrops onto the handle?

 **Gross Motor Skills**

Blow up a balloon and call out a number from **2** to **7**. Can you and your child toss the balloon in the air that many times without letting it hit the ground?

Invent letter races to do with your child. For letter **n**, can you push a nickel with your nose across a table? For letter **w**, can you wiggle on your belly like a worm across the room?

 Seasonal Fun

Make latkes with your child to celebrate Hanukkah. Grate eight large potatoes and one large onion and strain to remove liquid. Combine with two egg yolks, two tablespoons flour, and salt and pepper to taste. Beat two egg whites and fold in gently. Heat vegetable oil and fry the potato pancakes, turning them when they are crisp and golden brown.

Find a recipe for homemade play dough. Make it with your child and divide the batch in two. Knead green food coloring and a few drops of peppermint oil into one batch. Knead red food coloring and a few drops of cinnamon oil into the other batch. Let your child use cookie cutters with the dough to make Christmas shapes.

Week 10 Skills

Subject	Skill	Multi-Sensory Learning Activities
Reading and Language Arts	Recognize and write the letters **S** and **s**.	• Complete Practice Pages 112 and 113. • Use play dough to make two slithering snakes shaped like **S** and **s**. Bake at 250° for several hours until hardened. Then, use paint to add features. Have your child use a finger to trace the shapes from top to bottom.
	Recognize and write the letters **T** and **t**.	• Complete Practice Pages 114 and 115. • Make a cup of very strong tea. Let your child dip a paintbrush into the tea and paint **T** and **t** on construction paper.
Math	Distinguish between two-dimensional and three-dimensional (solid) shapes.	• Complete Practice Page 117. • On a trip to the discount store, challenge your child to find things shaped like a cube (example: a box), a cone (example: a party hat), and a sphere (example: a basketball). • Collect an assortment of discarded boxes and packages. Talk about how they are three-dimensional, or solid, shapes. Help your child glue them together to make a sculpture.
	Combine simple shapes.	• Complete Practice Pages 118 and 119. • Play with the tangrams from page 119. Can your child use them to make a boat? A house? Let your child suggest things for you to build, too.

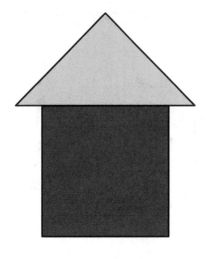

Letter Ss

UPPERCASE

lowercase

These pictures begin with the letter **S**, **s**. Color the pictures.

Letter Ss

Look at the letter patterns on the shirts and shorts. Draw a line from each shirt to the pair of shorts with the same letter pattern.

Letter Tt

UPPERCASE

lowercase

These pictures begin with the letter **T**, **t**. Color the pictures.

Letter Tt

Trace the letters **T** and **t** on the turkey's feathers below.
Then, cut out the feathers and glue them on the turkey.

Geometry

Draw a red line under two-dimensional shapes. Draw a blue line under three-dimensional objects.

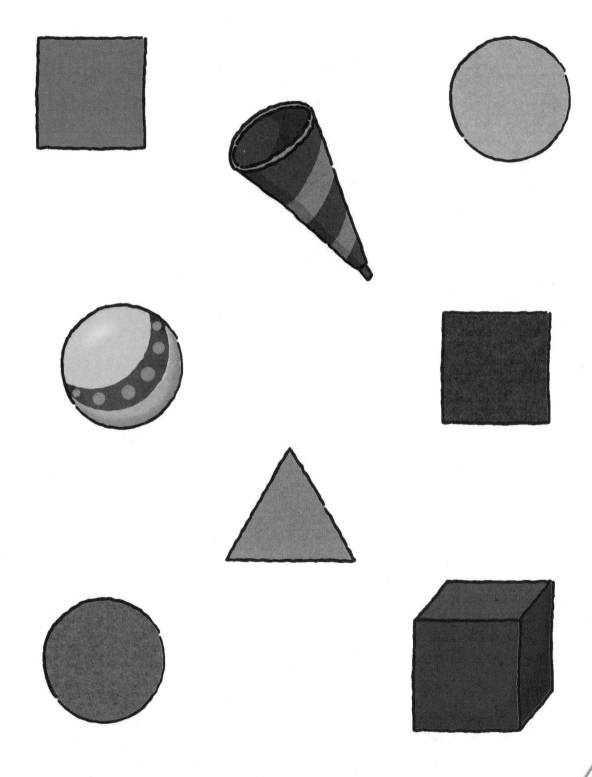

Shapes

Trace the triangles.

What shape did you form? _____

_____

Trace the rectangles.

What shape did you form? _____

Geometry

Cut out the tangram below. Mix up the pieces. Try to put them back together into a square.

Week 11 Skills

Subject	Skill	Multi-Sensory Learning Activities
Reading and Language Arts	Recognize and write the letters **U** and **u**.	• Complete Practice Pages 122 and 123. • Write **happy**, **do**, **fair**, and **fold**. Ask your child to write **un** in front of each word to make a new word. Have your child point to **u** in each word, read the word, and tell what it means.
	Recognize and write the letters **V** and **v**.	• Complete Practice Pages 124 and 125. • Have your child paint **V** and **v** on construction paper using a vegetable, such as a carrot or celery stick, dipped in finger paint.
Math	Explore measurement by thinking about what is longer or shorter.	• Complete Practice Pages 127 and 128. • Ask your child to find something that is longer or shorter than his or her hand. What is longer or shorter than his or her whole arm? • Have your child guess what item in the room you are thinking of. Give clues that include the words **longer** and **shorter**. For example, say, "It is shorter than a banana." Take turns giving clues and guessing.
Basic Skills	Understand opposites short/tall and big/small.	• Complete Practice Pages 129 and 130. • Play "Opposites Charades." Act out opposites such as high/low or hot/cold. Can your child guess the opposite words? Take turns acting and guessing.

Letter Uu

UPPERCASE

lowercase

These pictures begin with the letter **U**, **u**. Color the pictures.

Letter Uu

Blast off to the Moon! Trace the **Uu** letter path to send the rocket up into outer space.

Letter Vv

UPPERCASE

lowercase

These pictures begin with the letter **V**, **v**. Color the pictures.

COMPLETE YEAR KINDERGARTEN

Letter Vv

Help finish the flowers in the vase. Trace the letter **V** on each circle below. Then, cut out the circles and glue them in the middle of the flowers.

Longer

Look at the snake. Draw a longer snake below it.

Shorter

Look at the top wagon. Draw a shorter handle on the bottom wagon.

Short and Tall

Circle each short person below. Draw a line under each tall person.

Big and Small

Color the big shape in each box. Draw a line under the small shape in each box.

Week 12 Skills

Subject	Skill	Multi-Sensory Learning Activities
Reading and Language Arts	Recognize and write the letters **W** and **w**.	• Complete Practice Pages 132 and 133. • Mix finger paint with a small amount of dish soap. Let your child use the mixture to paint **W** and **w** on a window. It will wash off easily. • Go on a hunt at your home to find these things that begin with **w**: washcloth, water, watch, wallet, wheel.
	Recognize and write the letters **X** and **x**.	• Complete Practice Pages 134 and 135. • Show your child how to form **X** by crossing two arms and **x** by crossing two fingers. • Look for EXIT signs at stores and restaurants. Ask your child to name the letters on the signs.
Math	Explore measurement by thinking about length, height, and size.	• Complete Practice Pages 136–140. • Have your child make awards to present to his or her stuffed animals, dolls, or action figures. Awards should include tallest, shortest, smallest, and biggest. • Cut a length of string or yarn. Ask your child to find something in your home that is about that same length.
Bonus: Gross Motor Skills		• Play "Simon Says" with your child. Use these **w** words in your commands: **wink**, **wiggle**, **whisper**, **wave**, **waddle**, **walk**, **whine**, **whistle**, **whirl**.

Letter Ww

UPPERCASE

lowercase

These pictures begin with the letter **W**, **w**. Color the pictures.

Letter Ww

Look at the letters. Circle the animals with the letter **Ww**.

Letter Xx

UPPERCASE

lowercase

These pictures have the letter **X**, **x**. Color the pictures.

COMPLETE YEAR KINDERGARTEN

Letter Xx

Say the names of the pictures below. Then, trace the **x** to complete each word.

fo

bo

o

Long and Short

Circle each long thing. Then, draw a line under each short thing.

Same Size

Circle the shape in each row that is the same size as the first shape.

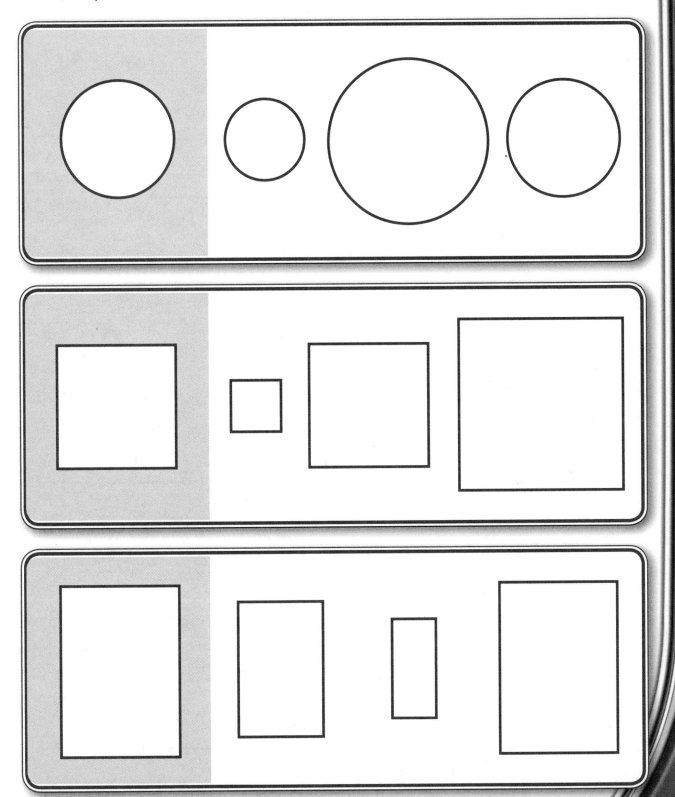

Same Size

Circle the shape in each row that is the same size as the first shape.

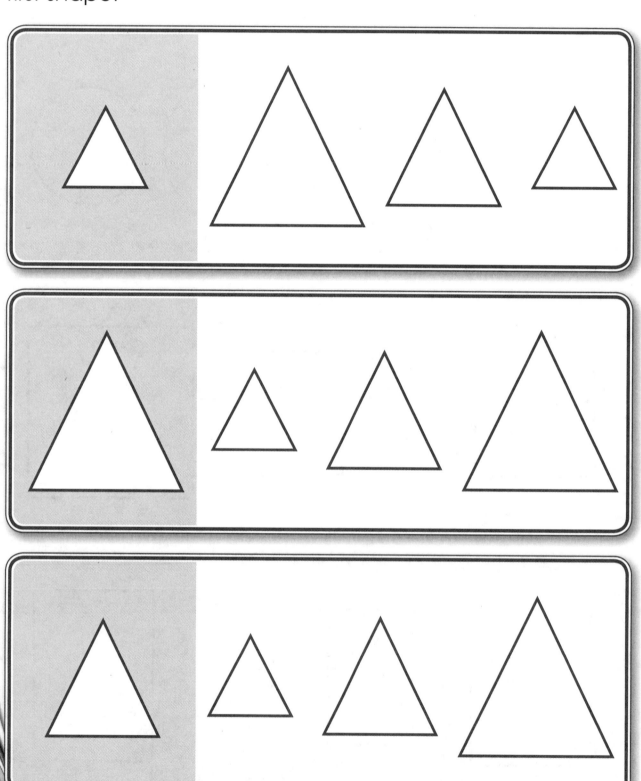

Review Size

Color the longest crayon red. Color the shortest crayon purple.

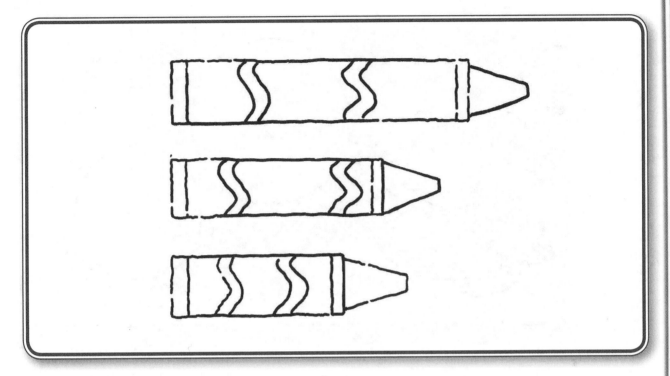

Circle the two bears that are the same size.

Review Size

Color the biggest ball blue. Color the smallest ball green.

Draw a line under the shortest tree. Circle the tallest tree.

Week 13 Skills

Subject	Skill	Multi-Sensory Learning Activities
Reading and Language Arts	Recognize and write the letters **Y** and **y**.	• Complete Practice Pages 142 and 143. • Have your child glue yellow yarn to paper in the shape of **Y** and **y** and trace the yarn letters with a finger, starting at the top.
	Recognize and write the letters **Z** and **z**.	• Complete Practice Pages 144 and 145. • Purchase three zippers from the fabric store. Ask your child to arrange them in a **Z** shape, then unzip them from top to bottom to show how to form **Z**.
Basic Skills	Understand position words **above**, **below**, and **between**.	• Complete Practice Pages 147 and 148. • Hide a small surprise. Help your child find it by giving clues that include the words **above**, **below**, and **between**.
Math	Recognize, write, and count the number **0**.	• Complete Practice Pages 149 and 150. • Ask your child to bring you specific numbers of items such as two apples, four napkins, or zero tomatoes. Help your child understand that zero means "none."
Bonus: Fine Motor Skills		• Draw a circle outline on plain paper and spread glue inside. Let your child fill the circle with a long spiral of yarn to make a yo-yo picture.

Letter Yy

UPPERCASE

lowercase

These pictures begin with the letter **Y**, **y**. Color the pictures.

Letter Yy

Color to find the hidden picture. Color the spaces with **Y** yellow. Color the other spaces orange.

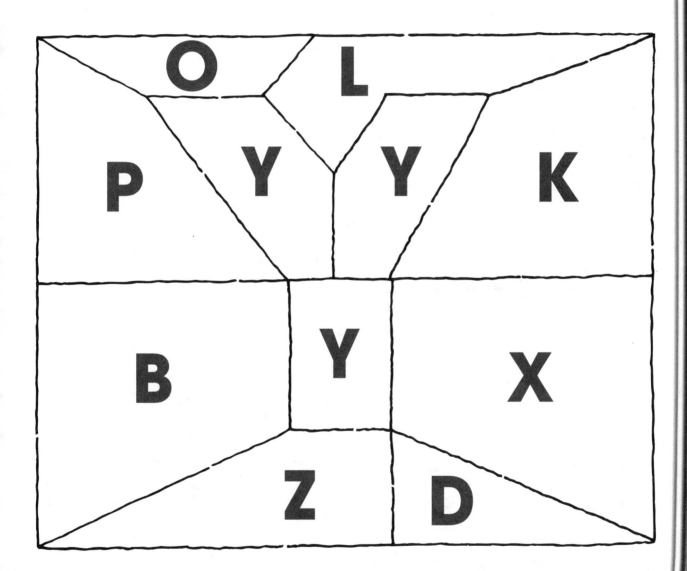

What did you find? _____

Letter Zz

UPPERCASE

lowercase

These pictures begin with the letter **Z**, **z**. Color the pictures.

Letter Zz

These zippers need zipper pulls. Cut out the pictures below that have the letter **Zz**. Then, glue them on the zipper pulls.

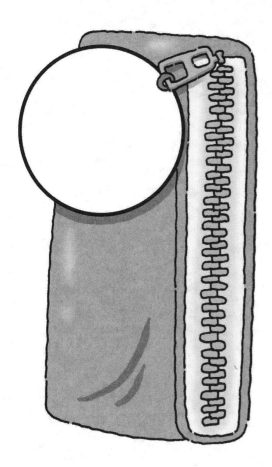
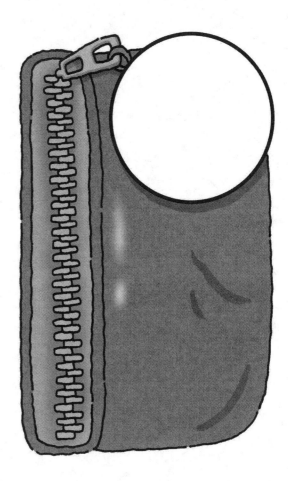

- -

Above and Below

Look at the picture. Circle the pictures above the bird.
Draw an **X** on the pictures below the bird.

Between

Color each shape that is between the other shapes.

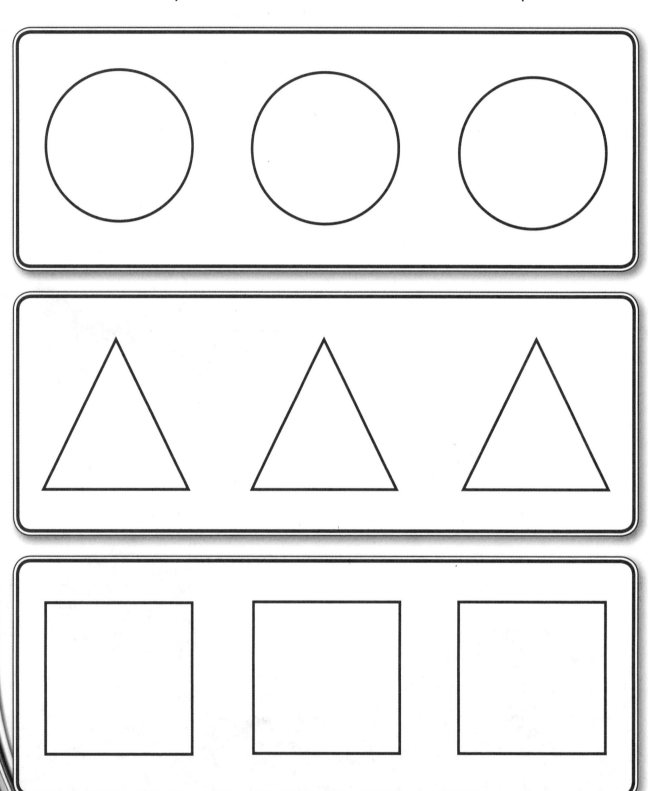

Number 0

The hungry kittens ate all the food in some bowls. Color the food bowls that have **0** food in them.

Practice writing the number **0**.

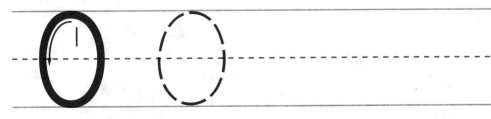

0 Zero

Color the fish with **0** spots orange.

Week 14 Skills

Subject	Skill	Multi-Sensory Learning Activities
Reading and Language Arts	Match uppercase and lowercase letters.	• Complete Practice Pages 152 and 153. • Write uppercase letters **A–Z** on one set of index cards and lowercase letters **a–z** on a second set of cards. Shuffle all the cards and use them to play "Memory" with your child.
	Review letters **Aa–Zz**.	• Complete Practice Pages 154–156. • Use the cards created for the "Memory" game described above. Can your child put the cards in alphabetical order? • Read a favorite picture book together. Can your child look at the words in the book and find all 26 letters of the alphabet?
Math	Recognize, write, and count the number **1**.	• Complete Practice Pages 157 and 158. • Take a tour through your home, pointing out things that you only have one of. For each, say "one." • Provide a bag of candies, raisins, or crackers. Ask your child to count one piece of food. Then, ask him or her to count "one more." Count the total each time "one more" is added.
	Recognize, write, and count the number **2**.	• Complete Practice Pages 159 and 160. • Have your child name body parts that come in pairs. For each pair of parts, count "one, two." • Hide the magnetic number **2** inside your child's shoe. Say this rhyme to help your child find it: Two, two/How are you?/You look so comfy/In my shoe! Encourage your child to think of more number rhymes.

Alphabet Review

Draw a line to match each UPPERCASE letter with the correct lowercase letter.

C		g
G		m
B		e
K		c
E		j
M		b
J		k
H		a
L		i
A		h
F		d
I		l
D		f

Alphabet Review

Draw a line to match each UPPERCASE letter with the correct lowercase letter.

R			v
N			r
Y			u
V			n
O			x
X			y
U			o
Z			w
S			z
P			t
W			p
Q			s
T			q

Great Gumballs!

Connect the dots from **A** to **Z**. Color the gumballs your favorite colors!

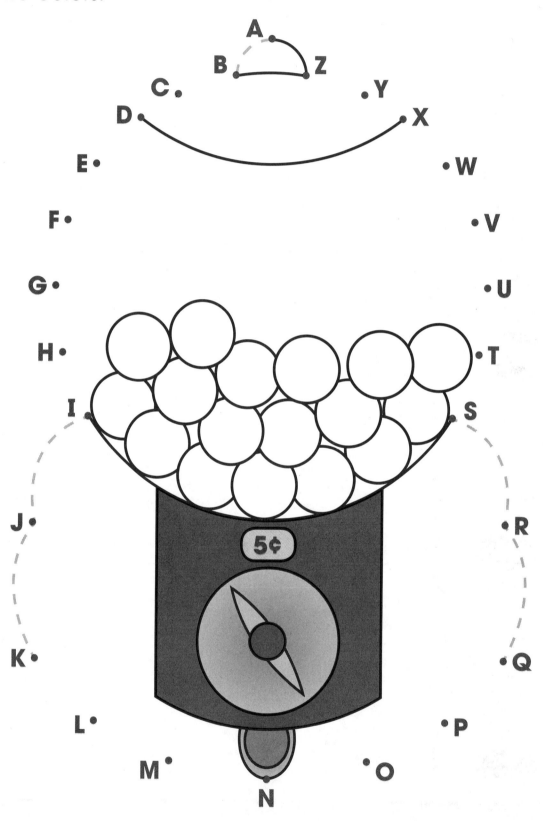

Review UPPERCASE Letters

Write the missing UPPERCASE letters to complete the alphabet.

Review Lowercase Letters

Write the missing lowercase letters to complete the alphabet.

Number 1

This is the number **1**. Color the picture.

How many things are in this picture? _____

Trace the 1s.

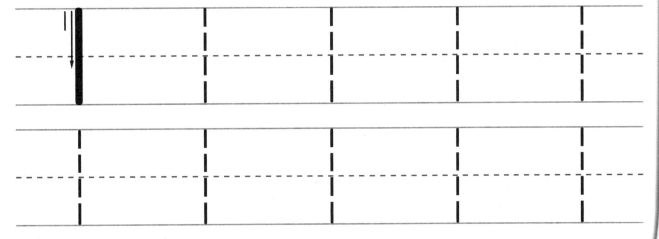

Write your own 1s.

_____

- -

_____

I One

Circle **I** picture in each box. Then, write the number **I** on the line in each box.

Number 2

This is the number **2**. Color the picture.

How many things are in this picture? _____

Trace the 2s.

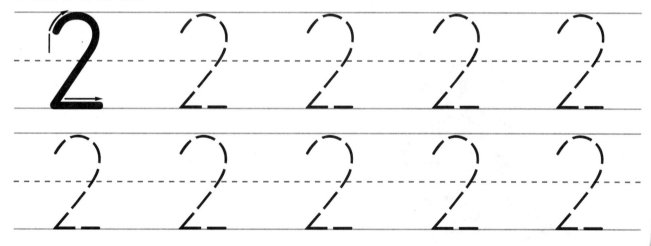

Write your own 2s.

_____

- -

_____

2 Two

Draw another picture in each box to make 2 of each thing.

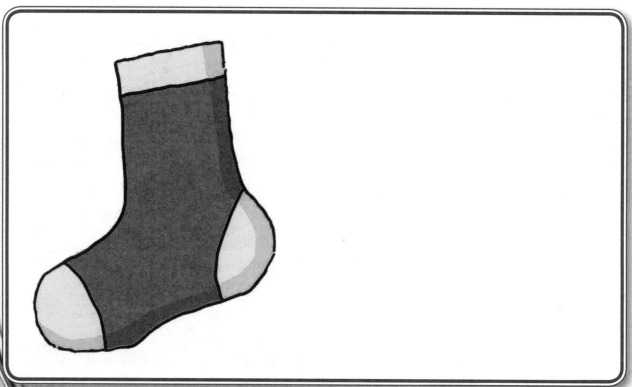

Week 15 Skills

Subject	Skill	Multi-Sensory Learning Activities
Reading and Language Arts	Associate the /**b**/ sound with letter **b**.	• Complete Practice Page 162. • Blow soap bubbles for your child. For each bubble, challenge him or her to say a word that begins with **b** before it pops!
	Associate the /**k**/ sound with letter **c**.	• Complete Practice Page 163. • Toss a cap into the air. Before it falls to the floor, challenge your child to say a word that begins with **c** and catch it.
	Associate the /**d**/ sound with letter **d**.	• Complete Practice Page 165. • Have your child stand on the top step of a stairway and say this rhyme: Downstairs, downstairs, d-d-d/I have a word that starts with **d**! Your child must say a **d** word before taking each step down.
	Associate the /**f**/ sound with letter **f**.	• Complete Practice Page 166. • Tell your child you will draw only pictures that begin with **f**. Then, begin to draw each of these objects while your child tries to guess what it is: farmer, fox, face, fish, fog, fairy, fan.
Math	Recognize, write, and count the number **3**.	• Complete Practice Pages 167 and 168. • Have your child fold a square piece of paper once lengthwise and once crosswise to form four smaller squares. Tell your child to color three of the squares.
	Recognize, write, and count the number **4**.	• Complete Practice Pages 169 and 170. • Give your child four pretzel sticks or dry spaghetti noodles. Can he or she use them to form the number **4**?

Beginning Consonant Bb

Say each picture name. If the picture name begins with the same sound as **ball**, color the space.

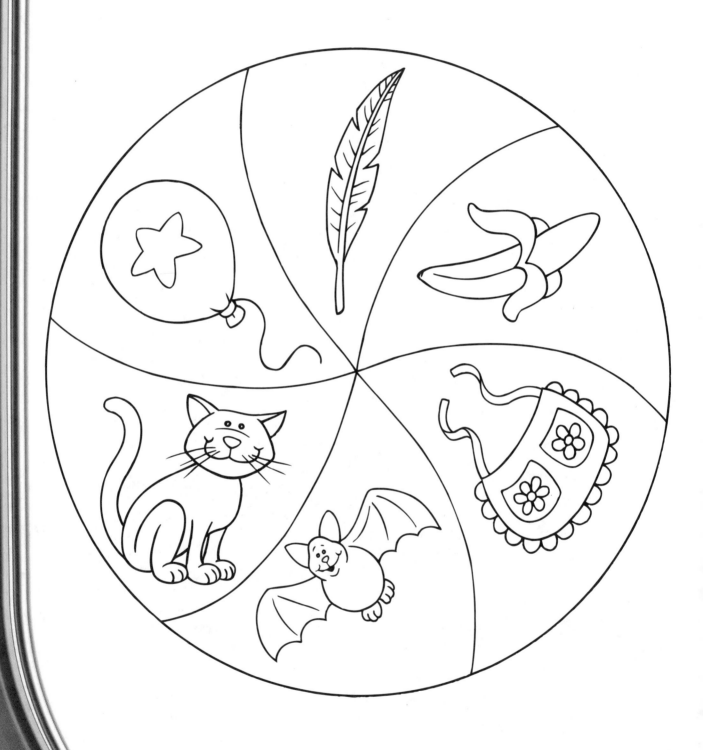

Beginning Consonant Cc

Cut out the pictures at the bottom. If the picture begins with the same sound as **caterpillar**, glue it on the caterpillar to give him some spots.

Beginning Consonant Dd

Say the picture names in each box on the door. Circle the picture whose name begins with the same sound as **dinosaur**.

Beginning Consonant Ff

Look at the bubbles below. Say each picture name. If the picture begins with the same sound as **fish**, color it blue.

Number 3

This is the number **3**. Color the picture.

How many things are in this picture? _____

Trace the 3s.

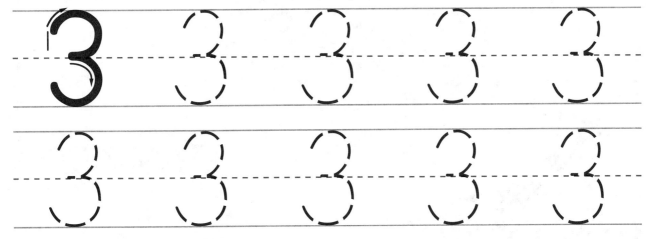

Write your own 3s.

_____

- -

_____

3 Three

Circle **3** of each kind of cookie to go in the cookie jar.

Number 4

This is the number **4**. Color the picture.

How many things are in this picture? _____

Trace the 4s.

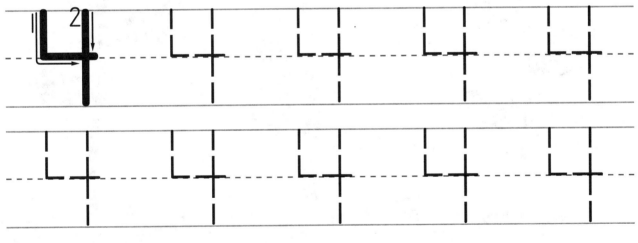

Write your own 4s.

_____

- -

_____

4 Four

Count the leaves on each flower. Draw more leaves so there are **4** on each stem. Trace and write **4** on the lines below.

_____   _____   _____

Week 16 Skills

Subject	Skill	Multi-Sensory Learning Activities
Reading and Language Arts	Associate the /**g**/ sound with letter **g**.	• Complete Practice Page 172. • Cut off the top of a gallon milk jug. Can your child fill the jug with small items that begin with **g**?
	Associate the /**h**/ sound with letter **h**.	• Complete Practice Page 173. • Play "Charades" with your child, taking turns acting out things that begin with **h** such as hen, horse, harp, hippo, and handshake.
	Associate the /**j**/ sound with letter **j**.	• Complete Practice Page 174. • Give clues to help your child guess **j** words such as **jacket** and **juice**. Begin with this rhyme: I know a **j** word, a **j** word, a **j** word/I know a **j** word/Do you want to play?
	Associate the /**k**/ sound with letter **k**.	• Complete Practice Page 175. • Explain that the /**k**/ sound can be spelled **c** or **k**. Help your child make a list of words that begin with **k**.
	Associate the /**l**/ sound with letter **l**.	• Complete Practice Page 176. • Eat lemonade and licorice. What other foods begin with **l**?
Math	Recognize, write, and count the number **5**.	• Complete Practice Pages 177 and 178. • Hold up a number of fingers on one hand. Ask your child, "How many more will make five?"
	Review numbers **1–5**.	• Complete Practice Pages 179 and 180. • Use your finger to trace a number from **0** to **5** on your child's back. Can he or she guess the number and clap that many times?

Beginning Consonant Gg

Say each picture name. Circle the pictures whose names begin with the same sound as **goggles**.

Beginning Consonant Hh

Say each picture name. If the picture begins with the **Hh** sound, color the hat.

Beginning Consonant Jj

What is Jamie wearing today? Say each picture name. Color the spaces with the **Jj** sound blue. Color the other spaces yellow.

What is Jamie wearing? _____

Beginning Consonant Kk

Look at the pictures on the kite's tail. Say each picture name. If the picture begins with the same sound as **kite**, color it orange. Then, color the kite.

Beginning Consonant Ll

Look at the stamps below. Say each picture name. If the picture begins with the same sound as **letter**, draw it on an envelope.

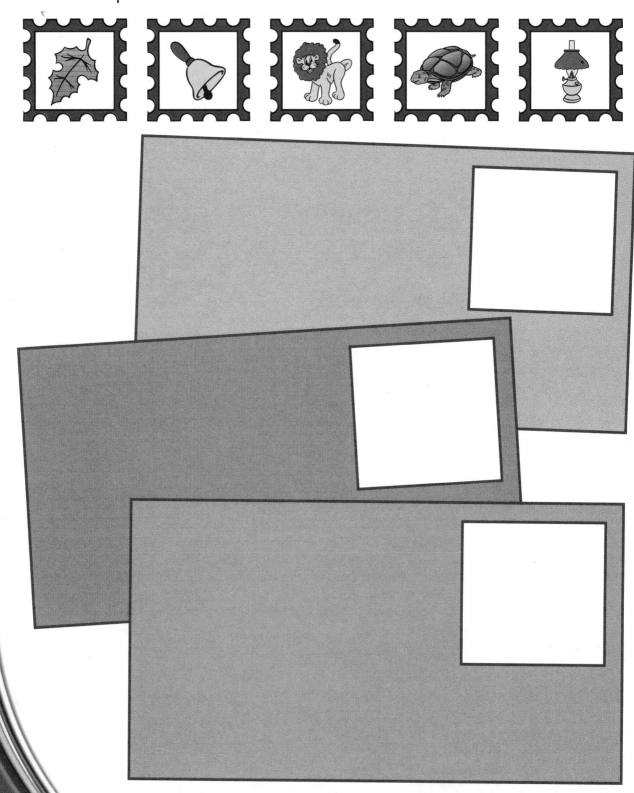

Number 5

This is the number **5**. Color the picture.

How many things are in this picture? _____

Trace the 5s.

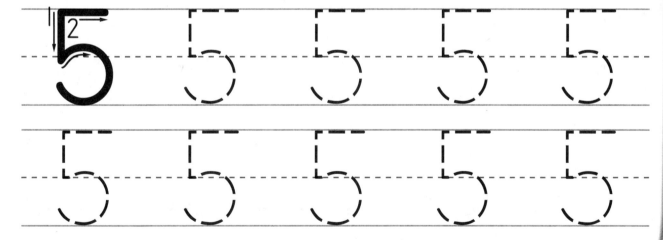

Write your own 5s.

_____

- -

_____

5 Five

Count the shapes. Then, color and decorate the butterfly.

How many ◯s? _____

How many △s? _____

How many ▢s? _____

Review Numbers 1–5

Look at the picture. Read the questions. Circle the correct number.

How many in all?   1   2   3

How many in all?   1   2   3

How many in all?   2   3   4

Review Numbers 1–5

Look at the picture. Read the questions. Circle the correct number.

How many in all?　　3　　4　　5

How many in all?　　3　　4　　5

How many in all?　　3　　4　　5

Week 17 Skills

Subject	Skill	Multi-Sensory Learning Activities
Reading and Language Arts	Associate the /**m**/ sound with letter **m**.	• Complete Practice Page 182. • Ask your child to fill a mitten with pictures of things that begin with **m**. Look at the pictures together, naming each one.
	Associate the /**n**/ sound with letter **n**.	• Complete Practice Page 183. • Say words such as **moon**, **noodle**, **pan**, **nurse**, and **wind**. Ask your child to nod when he or she hears a word that begins with **n**.
	Associate the /**p**/ sound with letter **p**.	• Complete Practice Page 184. • Have an indoor or outdoor picnic with paper plates, pickles, pears, and other **p** supplies.
	Associate the /**kw**/ sound with letter **q**.	• Complete Practice Page 185. • Help your child write a question that includes one or more **q** words. Remind him or her to end the sentence with a question mark.
	Associate the /**r**/ sound with letter **r**.	• Complete Practice Page 186. • Race against your child to see how many **r** objects each of you can find in two minutes. Items may include ribbon, remote controls, or raisins.
Math	Review numbers **1–5**.	• Complete Practice Pages 187 and 188. • Have your child illustrate a little book with zero children on the first page, one child on the second page, two children holding hands on the third page, etc. Write a number on each page. Flip through the book to see the number of friends grow.
	Recognize, write, and count the number **6**.	• Complete Practice Pages 189 and 190. • Roll a die. Can your child write a number to represent each roll?

Beginning Consonant Mm

Say each picture name. Color the pictures whose names begin with the same sound as **macaroni** and **meatballs**.

Beginning Consonant Nn

Help the birds find their nest. Follow the path with the pictures whose names begin with the same sound as **nest**.

Beginning Consonant Pp

Pam only packs things whose names begin with the same sound as **panda**. Say the picture names. Circle each picture whose name begins with the same sound as **Pam** and **panda**.

Beginning Consonant Qq

Look at the pictures on the quilt below. Say each picture name. If the picture begins with the same sound as **quilt**, color the square yellow. Color the other squares purple.

Beginning Consonant Rr

Who is the raccoon going to visit? Say each picture name. Color the pictures whose names begin with the same sound as **raccoon**.

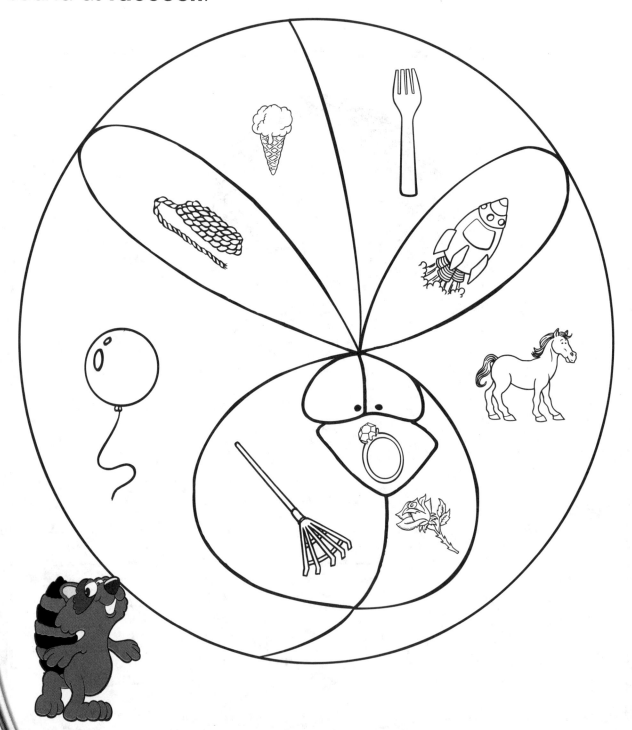

Who is the raccoon going to visit? _____

Review Numbers 1–5

Count the balloons. Then, write the correct number on the line.

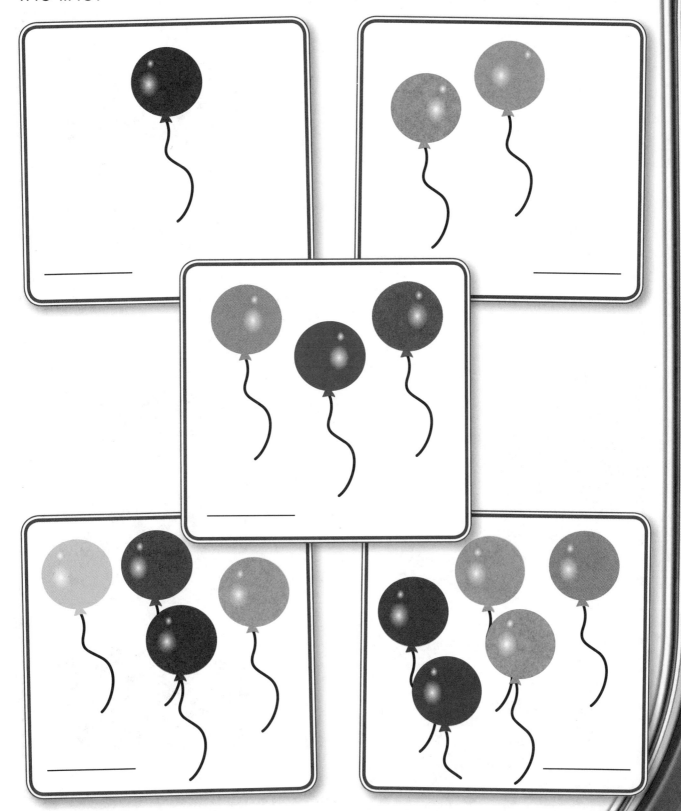

Review Numbers 1–5

Draw a line from the number to the group that matches.

1

2

3

4

5

Number 6

This is the number **6**. Color the picture.

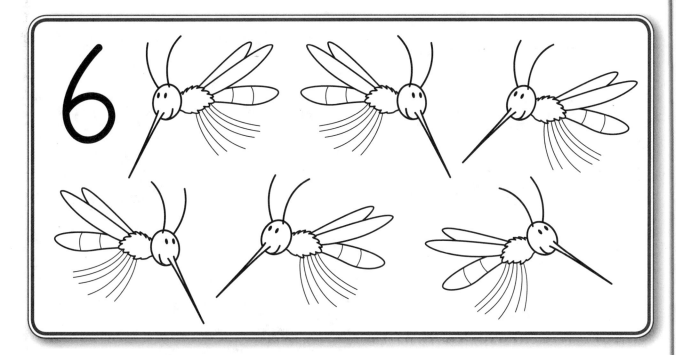

How many things are in this picture? _____

Trace the 6s.

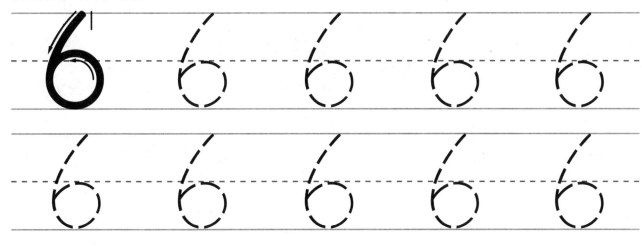

Write your own 6s.

_____

_____

6 Six

Circle 6 things in each box. Write the number **6** on each line.

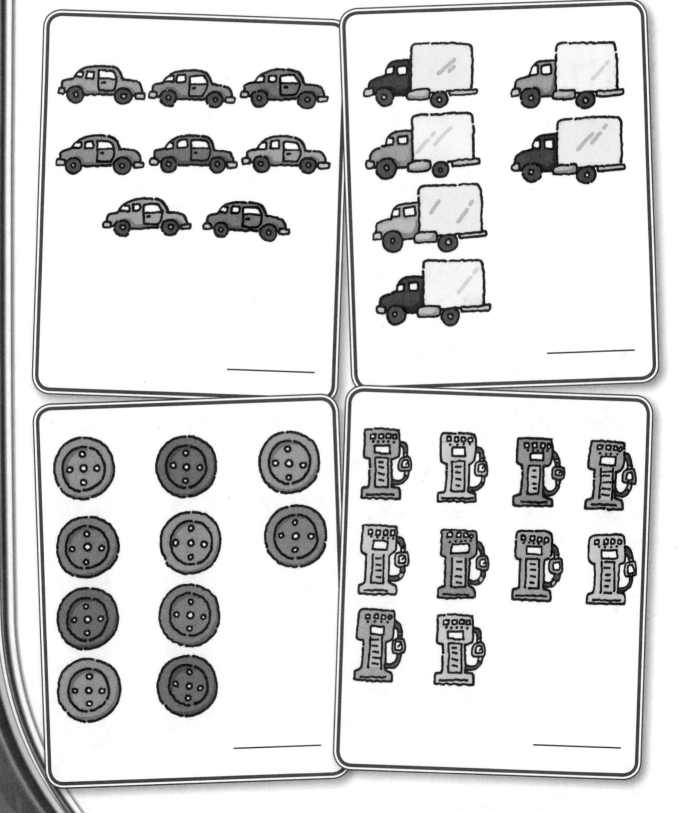

Week 18 Skills

Subject	Skill	Multi-Sensory Learning Activities
Reading and Language Arts	Associate the /**s**/ sound with letter **s**.	• Complete Practice Page 192. • Sam's going to San Diego and in his suitcase he'll pack a sandwich. Ask your child to repeat this sentence, adding something else to be packed that begins with **s**, such as sunscreen. Take turns repeating the sentence and adding **s** items until one of you makes a mistake.
	Associate the /**t**/ sound with letter **t**.	• Complete Practice Page 193. • Spin a top. Challenge your child to say words that begin with **t** until it stops.
	Associate the /**v**/ sound with letter **v**.	• Complete Practice Page 194. • Draw a vine on plain paper. On each leaf, have your child write a word that begins with **v**.
	Associate the /**w**/ sound with letter **w**.	• Complete Practice Page 195. • Read *Where the Wild Things Are* by Maurice Sendak. Find words in the story that begin with **w**.
	Associate the /**ks**/ sound with letter **x**.	• Complete Practice Page 196. • Have your child repeat these words that end with **x**, emphasizing the /**ks**/ sound: **box**, **fox**, **mix**, **fix**, **wax**.
Math	Review numbers **1–6**.	• Complete Practice Pages 197 and 198. • Provide an old greeting card or a picture printed on cardstock. Have your child cut it to make a jigsaw puzzle with six pieces. Ask your child to write a number **1–6** on the back of each piece.
	Recognize, write, and count the number **7**.	• Complete Practice Pages 199 and 200. • Have your child write a large **7** on drawing paper and turn it into a creature with seven arms, seven eyes, seven spots, etc.

Beginning Consonant Ss

Find the letter **S**. Say each picture name. If the picture begins with the same sound as **six**, color the space blue. Color the other spaces orange.

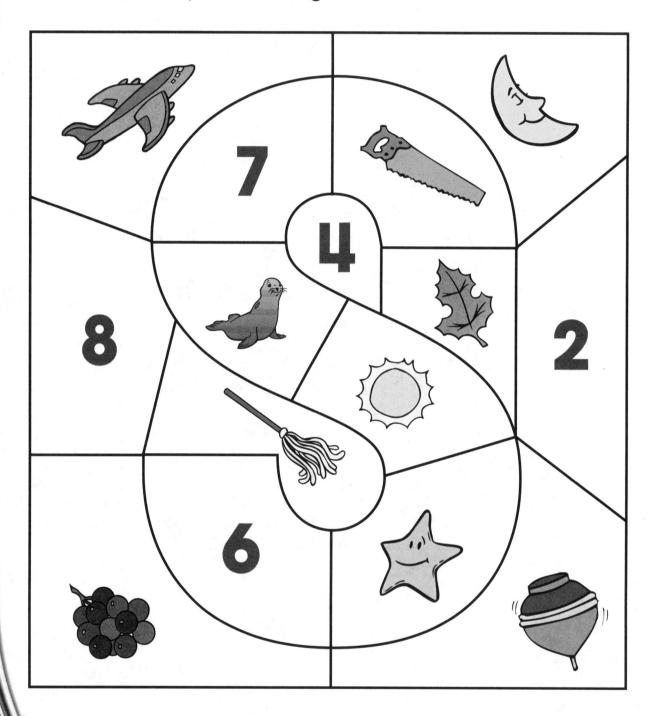

Beginning Consonant Tt

Say the picture name for each toy in the tub. Draw an **X** on the pictures whose names begin with the same sound as **tub**.

Beginning Consonant Vv

These pictures begin with the letter **Vv**. Color the pictures.

valentine

vase

vacuum

violin

Beginning Consonant Ww

These pictures begin with the letter **Ww**. Color the pictures.

wagon

watch

watermelon

window

Consonant Xx

Write **x** on the lines to complete each picture name. Then, color the big **X**.

e __ it

__ -ray

bo __

fo __

Review Numbers 1–6

Circle the correct number in each box.

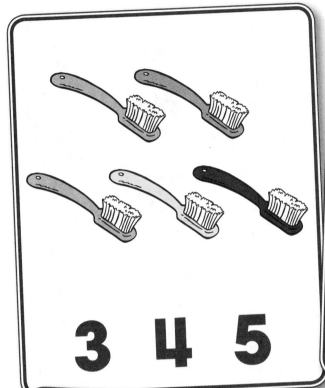

3 4 5

4 5 6

1 2 3

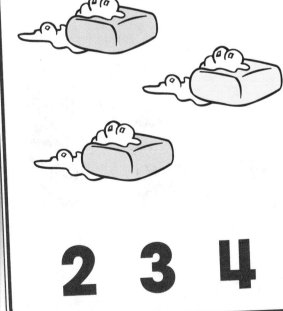

2 3 4

Review Numbers 1-6

Count each group of blocks. Trace each number. Then, count each group of blocks below. Write the number.

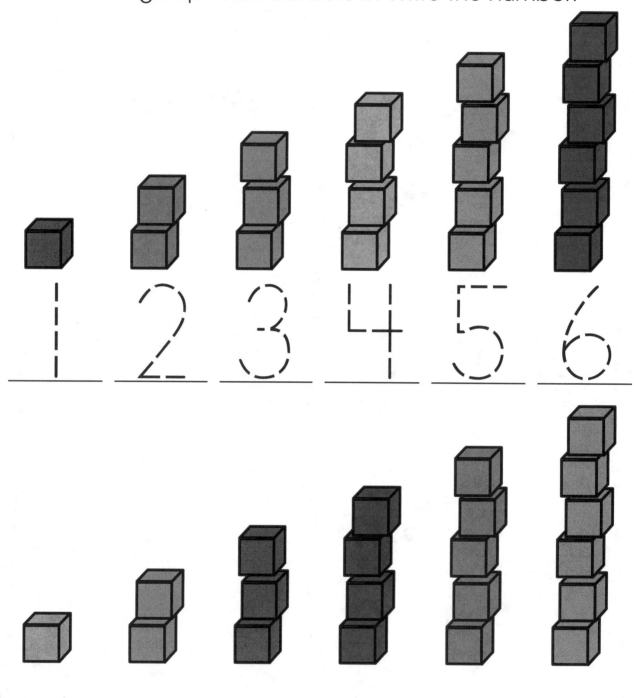

Number 7

This is the number **7**. Color the picture.

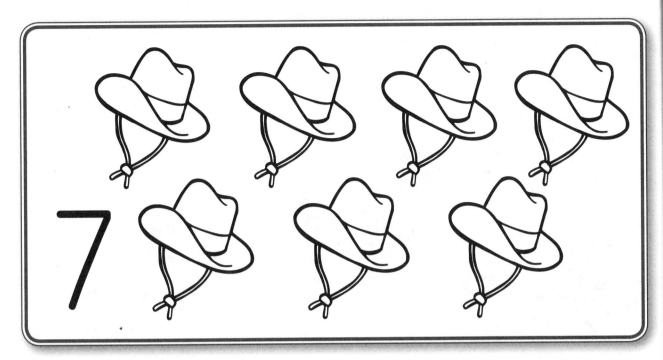

How many things are in this picture? _____

Trace the 7s.

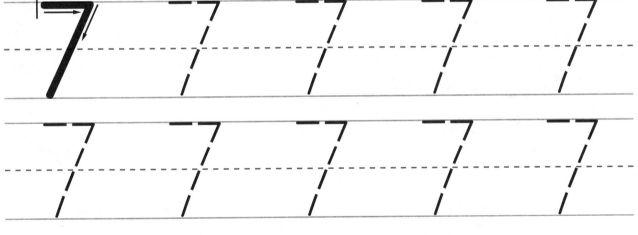

Write your own 7s.

---

7 Seven

Add some toppings to the pizza. Draw **7** pieces of pepperoni. Draw **7** mushrooms.

Second Quarter Check-Up

Basic Skills

❏ I know opposite pairs such as long/short and big/small.

❏ I know position words such as **above**, **below**, and **between**.

Reading and Language Arts

❏ I recognize all 26 uppercase letters.

❏ I recognize all 26 lowercase letters.

❏ I can write all 26 uppercase letters.

❏ I can write all 26 lowercase letters.

❏ I know the sounds made by these consonant letters: **b, c, d, f, g, h, j, k, l, m, n, p, q, r, s, t, v, w, x**.

Math

❏ I know the difference between two-dimensional and three-dimensional shapes.

❏ I recognize numbers **0–7**.

❏ I can write numbers **0–7**.

❏ I can count accurately to seven.

Final Project

Create a book or digital presentation about counting. A number and matching number word should appear at the top of each page. Choose a consonant sound to feature on each page, write a funny phrase that includes the sound, and draw a matching illustration. For example, if the number **4** page will feature the /**m**/ sound, you might write **monsters on a mattress** and draw four silly monsters bouncing on a bed.

Third Quarter Introduction

In the weeks after the winter or mid-year break, students are often ready to tackle new learning challenges. In many classrooms, brand-new concepts and skills are introduced during third quarter that may be difficult for your child. You can help at home by encouraging your child and providing positive learning support using resources found in *Complete Year*.

Third Quarter Skills

Practice pages in this book for Weeks 19–27 will help your child improve the following skills.

Basic Skills
- Understand the concepts **more** and **fewer**

Reading and Language Arts
- Identify sounds made by the consonant letters **y** and **z**
- Review consonant sounds
- Identify consonant sounds at the ends of words
- Identify the **short a** sound heard in **hat**
- Identify the **short e** sound heard in **hen**
- Identify the **short i** sound heard in **hit**
- Identify the **short o** sound heard in **hot**
- Identify the **short u** sound heard in **hut**
- Review short vowel sounds

Math
- Recognize numbers **8–20**
- Write numbers **8–20**
- Count up to 20 objects
- Compare numbers to tell which is greater

Multi-Sensory Learning Activities

Try these fun activities for enhancing your child's learning and development during the third quarter of the school year. Be sure to choose activities that include speaking, listening, touching, and active movement.

Basic Skills

Reinforce the concepts of **more** and **fewer** during everyday experiences. When folding laundry into stacks, ask which stack has more clothes and which has fewer. When spooning food onto your plate and your child's plate, ask who has more and who has less. The more opportunities you take to use these terms, the better your child will understand them and the more skilled he or she will become at estimating quantities.

 Reading and Language Arts

Provide a set of alphabet magnets for your child to use on the refrigerator, a cookie sheet, or another metallic surface. Say a three-letter word such as **man, pat, bed, let, fin, lit, hop, job, rug,** or **bus**, emphasizing each individual sound. Then, challenge your child to choose a magnetic letter to represent each sound in the word. Praise your child for correctly selecting letters for one, two, or all three of the sounds in the word! Help your child write three-letter words on paper, too.

Point out to your child that all words contain vowel letters **a, e, i, o, u**, and sometimes **y**. You can't spell a word without a vowel sound! Look through a favorite picture book with your child. Closely examine a number of words on the pages to confirm that each contains at least one vowel letter. Emphasize the importance of vowels by singing this song to the tune of "Twinkle, Twinkle, Little Star."

A, E, I, O, U, and **Y**
Are unique, I wonder why.
Is it 'cause each word needs you?

Look at that—I see it's true.
A, E, I, O, U, and **Y**
Are unique and I know why!

 Math

Have your child make a chart to show numbers **0–20**. Write the numbers from left to right across the bottom of a large sheet of paper. Then, in a stack above each number, draw circles or pictures or attach stickers to show the corresponding number.

Third Quarter Introduction, cont.

Use masking tape to make a giant number line on the floor. Divide the line into equal sections and label them with numbers **0–20**. Invite your child to walk and jump along the line as he or she counts to 20 by ones, fives, or tens.

Let your child help you measure and mix ingredients to make a batch of homemade play dough. Then, help your child roll the dough into 32 long tubes. Challenge your child to shape the tubes into numbers **0–20**. Ask your child to arrange the numbers in order.

Play with pennies and dimes. Explain that each dime equals 10 pennies. Call out a number from **11–19**. How many pennies need to be added to one dime to make that many cents?

 **Fine Motor Skills**

Let your child use a plastic knife to cut bite-sized chunks of fruits, vegetables, and cheese. Then, provide toothpicks and show how to use them to connect the pieces and build a tower, vehicle, or creature. Count the number of pieces used to make each sculpture. Then, enjoy a snack!

 **Gross Motor Skills**

Play "Animal Charades." Pretend to be an animal through movement and sounds. As a clue, tell your child the first letter in the animal's name. Can your child guess the animal? Take turns.

 Seasonal Fun

Search the Internet for two photos of winter scenes. Size the photos so that your child can view them at the same time. Invite your child to describe similarities and differences between the two photos.

Make a winter sun-catcher. Arrange short pine branches, sliced oranges, berries, and other natural items in the bottom of a disposable foil pan. Fill the pan halfway with water, covering the items. Submerge each end of a long length of twine to form a hanger. Freeze outside or in the freezer. Gently release the sun-catcher from the pan, running warm water on the back if needed. Hang it from a tree outside to sparkle in the sun!

Week 19 Skills

Subject	Skill	Multi-Sensory Learning Activities
Reading and Language Arts	Associate the /**y**/ sound with letter **y**.	• Complete Practice Page 206. • Say several words such as **water**, **yo-yo**, **under**, **yellow**, **noodle**, **yard**, **yawn**, and **wagon**. Ask your child to shout "Yeah!" when he or she hears the /**y**/ sound.
	Associate the /**z**/ sound with letter **z**.	• Complete Practice Page 207. • Listen to the song "We're Going to the Zoo" by Raffi. Sing along, raising your volume each time you sing the /**z**/ sound in **zoo**.
	Review consonant sounds.	• Complete Practice Pages 208–210. • Read a favorite alphabet book such as *LMNO Peas* by Keith Baker. Open to a random page. Can your child identify the letter, trace it with his or her finger, and name something that begins with the sound?
Math	Recognize, write, and count the number **8**.	• Complete Practice Pages 211 and 212. • Draw a web with eight rings. Glue on pictures of spiders printed from the Internet. Count the legs on each spider.
	Recognize, write, and count the number **9**.	• Complete Practice Pages 213 and 214. • Roll a pair of dice 20 times. Keep a tally to show how many times the roll equals nine.
Bonus: Gross Motor Skills		• Exercise with eight! Do eight jumping jacks, eight frog jumps, eight kicks, and eight side-steps.

Beginning Consonant Yy

Say each picture name. Draw a green line from each ball of yarn to the picture that begins with the **Yy** sound.

Beginning Consonant Zz

The word **zero** begins with the letter **Zz**. Complete the picture of the zero below.

zero

Review Beginning Consonants

Say each picture name. Circle the letter that stands for the beginning sound.

r   n   m   f   k   b

l   h   s   w   d   m

n   d   l   p   y   w

Review Beginning Consonants

Look at the letter in each box. Circle the picture that begins with that sound.

Review Beginning Consonants

Say the sound the letter makes. Circle the pictures in each row that begin with the letter shown.

COMPLETE YEAR KINDERGARTEN

Number 8

This is the number **8**. Color the picture.

How many things are in this picture? _____

Trace the 8s.

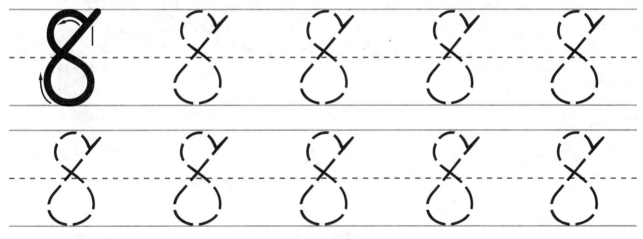

Write your own 8s.

_____

_____

_____

8 Eight

Draw a line from each basket to the tree with the same number of apples.

Number 9

This is the number **9**. Color the picture.

How many things are in this picture? _____

Trace the 9s.

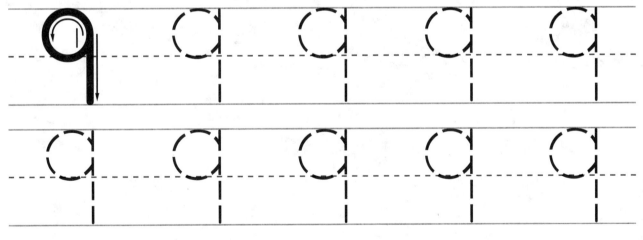

Write your own 9s.

_____

- -

_____

9 Nine

Help the bee get to the flower. Follow the path of numbers from **1** to **9**.

Week 20 Skills

Subject	Skill	Multi-Sensory Learning Activities
Reading and Language Arts	Review consonant sounds.	• Complete Practice Pages 216–219. • Help your child create a menu for the A–Z Café! Include a food item that begins with each letter of the alphabet. Write the menu inside a manila file folder.
Math	Recognize, write, and count the number **10**.	• Complete Practice Pages 221 and 222. • Have a snack of 10 crackers. How many ways can your child form two groups of crackers that add up to 10? • Hold up a number of fingers. Ask your child to hold up his or her fingers to show the number needed to make 10 altogether.
	Review numbers **6–10**.	• Complete Practice Pages 223 and 224. • Write numbers **0–10** on index cards. Illustrate the cards by drawing a matching number of objects. Write **+** and **=** signs on two more cards. Then, call out a number from **6–10**. Can your child use the cards to create an addition problem that equals that number? • When you are traveling in the car, look for objects to count. Count one bridge, two white houses, three dogs, four signs, etc.
Bonus: Fine Motor Skills		• Let your child cut lengths of yarn and tie a different number of knots in each piece. Can your child combine the pieces in different ways to get 10 knots?

Review Beginning Consonants

Say each picture name. Circle the beginning sound.

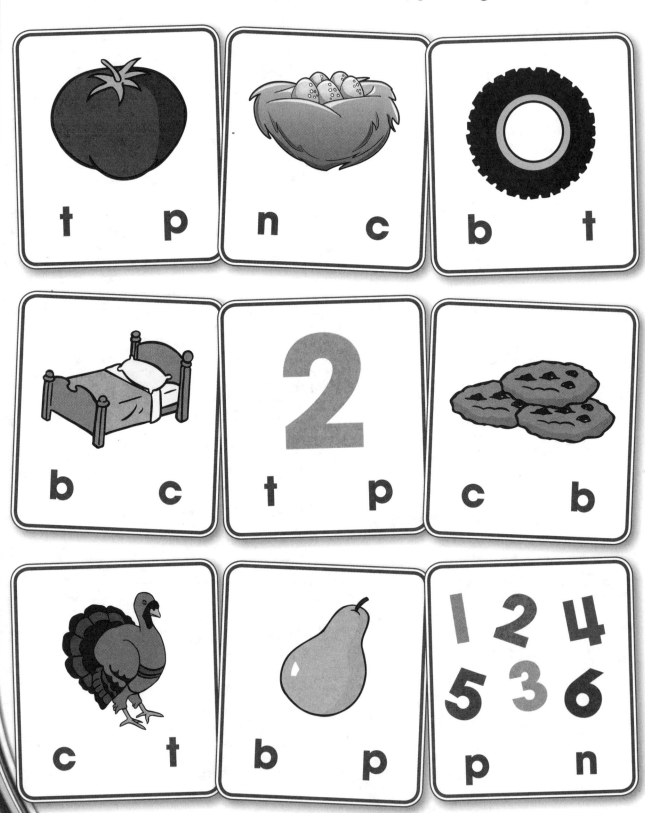

t p   n c   b t

b c   t p   c b

c t   b p   p n

COMPLETE YEAR KINDERGARTEN

Review Beginning Consonants

Say each picture name. Circle the beginning sound.

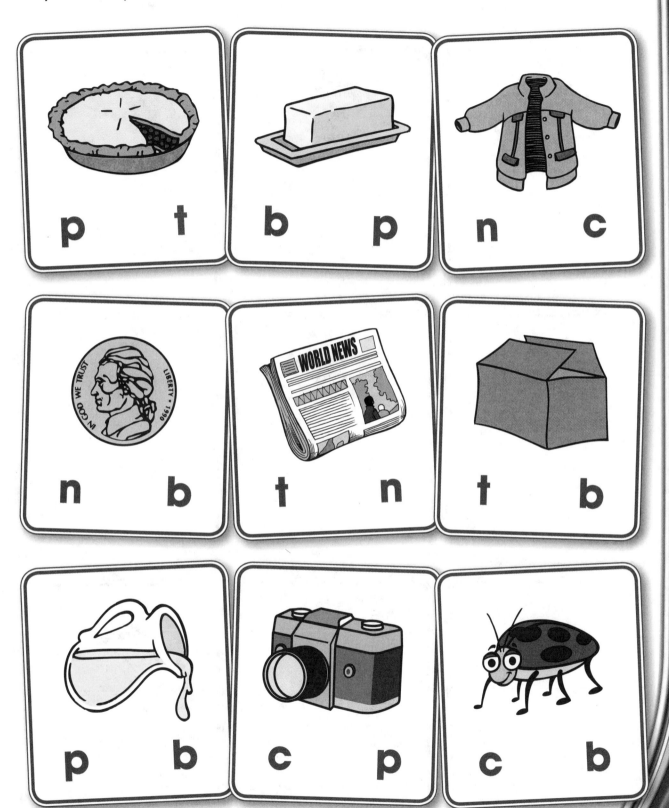

p   t   b   p   n   c

n   b   t   n   t   b

p   b   c   p   c   b

Review Beginning Consonants

Look at each picture. Write the beginning sound for each picture.

Review Beginning Consonants

Look at the letter in each column. Cut out each picture and glue it under the correct beginning sound.

Hh	Dd	Rr	Gg

Number 10

This is the number **10**. Color the picture.

How many things are in this picture? _____

Trace the 10s.

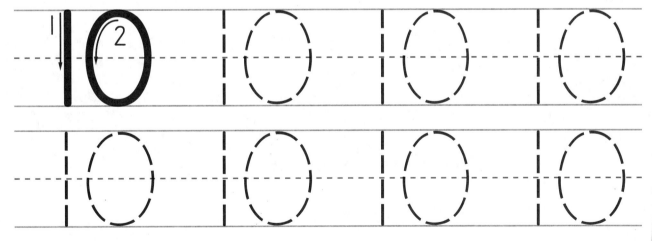

Write your own 10s.

_____

- -

_____

10 Ten

Draw **10** legs on the caterpillar.

Review 6–10

Count the number of dots on each hat. Write the number on the line.

Review Numbers 7–10

Circle the correct number in each box.

8   9   10

7   8   9

Week 21 Skills

Subject	Skill	Multi-Sensory Learning Activities
Reading and Language Arts	Identify consonant sounds at the ends of words.	• Complete Practice Pages 226–229. • Tape short lengths of yarn to join three jewelry box lids to form a "word train." Then, call out a three-letter word such as **man**, **pat**, **bed**, **let**, **fin**, **lit**, **hop**, **job**, **rug**, or **bus**. Can your child put a magnetic letter in each train car to spell the word? • Say a three-letter word, then touch either your head (for the first consonant), your belly (for the middle vowel), or your feet (for the final consonant). Can your child supply the letter you indicated?
Math	Review numbers **1–10**.	• Complete Practice Pages 230–233. • Make a ten frame by dividing a blank sheet of paper into two rows with five boxes in each row. Have your child count to 10 by putting a penny or other marker in each box. Then, fill only some of the boxes. How many more are needed to make 10?
	Compare numbers.	• Complete Practice Page 234. • Play the card game "War" with your child. Divide the deck, giving one facedown stack of cards to each player. Players turn over one card at a time. The higher number wins each hand.
Bonus: Gross Motor Skills		• Play "Hide and Seek" with your child. Model how to count to 100 by fives or tens before beginning to search.

5 10 15 20 25

Ending Consonant Sounds

Look at the picture in each box. Color the pictures in that row that end with the same sound.

226

Ending Consonant Sounds

Look at the picture in each box. Circle the pictures in that row that end with the same sound.

Ending Consonant Sounds

Look at the picture in each box. Circle the ending sound for each picture.

d   t   b   p   x   s

n   m   g   f   s   b

r   t   d   r   g   v

Ending Consonant Sounds

Say each picture name. Fill in the circle next to the ending sound.

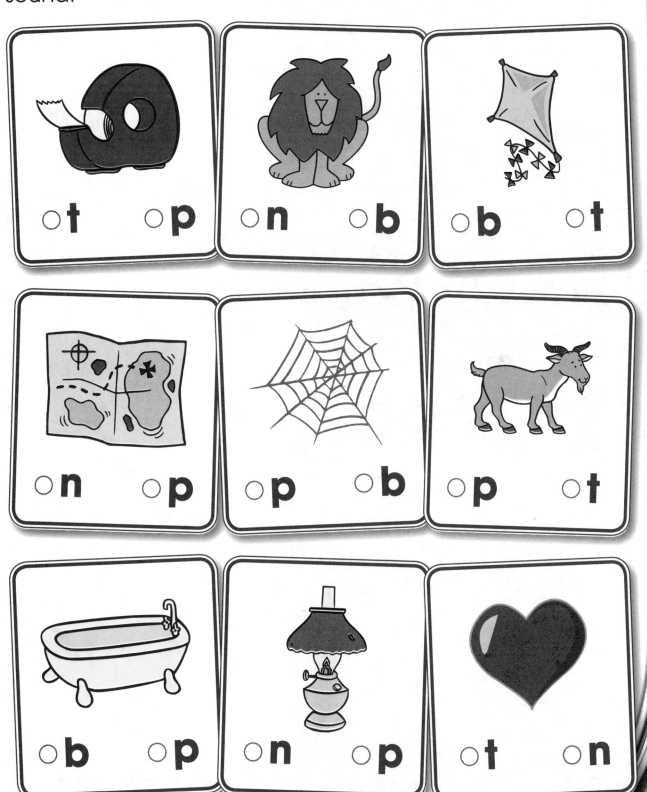

○ t   ○ p

○ n   ○ b

○ b   ○ t

○ n   ○ p

○ p   ○ b

○ p   ○ t

○ b   ○ p

○ n   ○ p

○ t   ○ n

Review Numbers 1–10

Connect the dots from **1** to **10**. Then, color the picture.

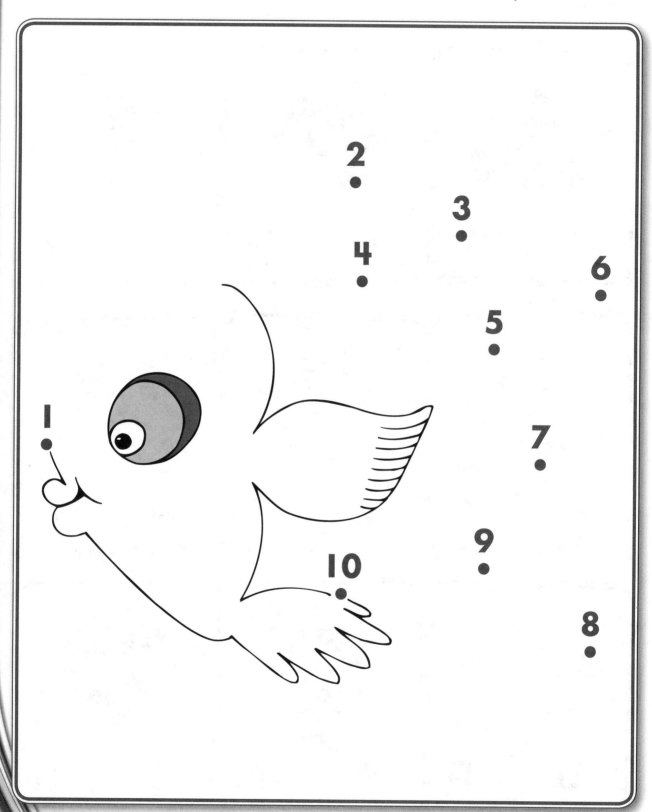

Review Numbers 1-10

Count your fingers on both hands. Write the numbers.

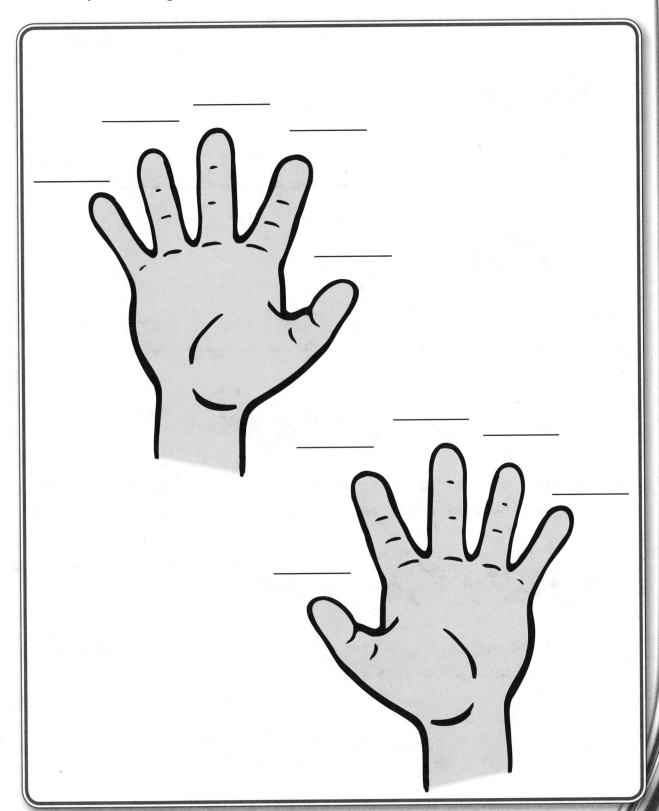

Review Numbers 1-10

Count the beads in each group. Write the number.

_____

_____

_____

_____

_____

COMPLETE YEAR KINDERGARTEN

Sequencing Numbers

Sequencing is putting numbers in the correct order.

1, 2, 3, 4, 5, 6, 7, 8, 9, 10

Write the missing numbers.

Example: 4, _____5_____, 6

3, _____, 5   7, _____, 9   8, _____, 10

6, _____, 8   _____, 3, 4   _____, 5, 6

5, 6, _____   _____, 6, 7   _____, 3, 4

_____, 4, 5   _____, 7, 8   5, _____, 7

2, 3, _____   1, 2, _____   7, 8 , _____

2, _____, 4   _____, 2, 3   4, _____, 6

6, 7, _____   3, 4, _____   1, _____, 3

7, 8, _____   _____, 3, 4   _____, 9, 10

Comparing Numbers

Circle the number that is larger in each pair.

4 2	2 6
6 5	1 2
7 1	9 5
9 6	1 3

Week 22 Skills

Subject	Skill	Multi-Sensory Learning Activities
Reading and Language Arts	Identify the **short a** vowel sound.	• Complete Practice Pages 236–239. • Clap hands with your child as you say the rhyme "Miss Mary Mack." Can your child pick out the **short a** words in the rhyme? • Spell **-at**, **-an**, or **-ap** with magnetic letters. Can your child add different consonants to make words? Say each word, emphasizing the **short a** sound.
Math	Recognize, write, and count the number **11**.	• Complete Practice Pages 240 and 241. • Count 11 coins, raisins, or other items. Put 10 in a bowl. Emphasize that 11 is 10 plus one more.
	Recognize, write, and count the number **12**.	• Complete Practice Pages 242 and 243. • Write a number **1–12** in the bottom of each cup of an empty egg carton. Have your child count out dry beans to fill the cups.
	Review numbers **1–12**.	• Complete Practice Page 244. • Examine an analog clock face with your child. Together, point to the numbers and count from 1–12.
Bonus: Fine Motor Skills		• Let your child help you make one dozen muffins or cupcakes. Ask him or her to count out 12 paper liners for the treats.

Short Vowel Aa

Short Aa is the sound at the beginning of the word **alligator**. Color the pictures that begin with the **short Aa** sound.

Short Vowel Aa

Short Aa is the sound at the beginning of the word **animals**. Say each picture name. Circle the pictures whose names have the **short Aa** sound.

Short Vowel Aa

Name each picture. Write the correct letter at the beginning of each word. The first one is done for you.

h   m

hat

c   d

at

b   p

at

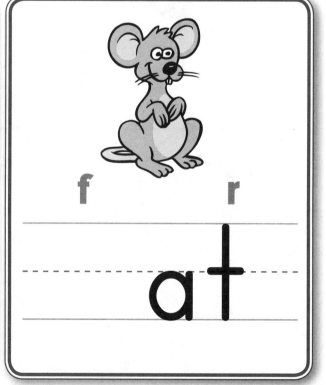

f   r

at

Short Vowel Aa

Read the words. Draw a line from each word to the picture that matches it.

bat   hat   cat

Number 11

This is the number **11**. Color the picture.

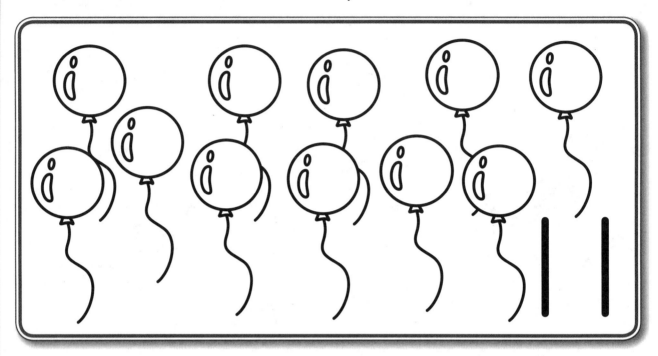

How many things are in this picture? _____

Trace the 11s.

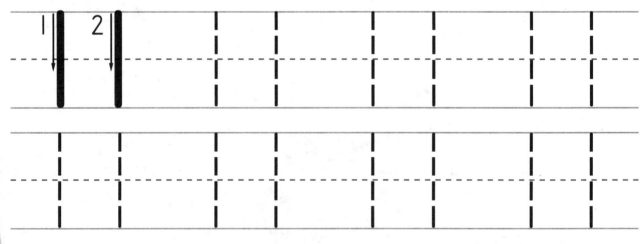

Write your own 11s.

_____

- -

_____

II Eleven

Count Zeb Zebra's stripes and color them.

Number 12

This is the number **12**. Color the picture.

How many things are in this picture? _____

Trace the 12s.

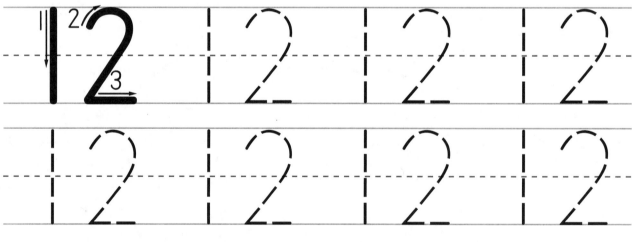

Write your own 12s.

_____

- -

_____

12 Twelve

Count each group of creatures. Draw a line from the creatures to their matching apples.

Review Numbers 1-12

Count the number of colored squares. Then, write the correct number.

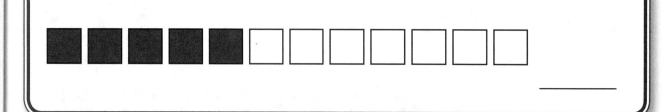

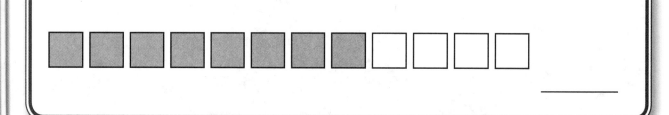

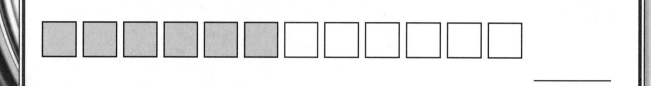

Week 23 Skills

Subject	Skill	Multi-Sensory Learning Activities
Reading and Language Arts	Identify the **short e** vowel sound.	• Complete Practice Pages 246–250. • The **short e** sound is heard at the beginning of **egg**. Say these words and ask your child to clap when he or she hears **short e**: **eleven, apple, elbow, egg, hat, hen, elephant**. • Write several three-letter words such as **man, hen, bed, let, fin, lit, hop, pen, rug**, and **bet** on slips of paper. Ask your child to choose only those with the **short e** sound to place inside an envelope.
Math	Recognize, write, and count the number **13**.	• Complete Practice Pages 251 and 252. • Make a stack of 10 interlocking blocks. How many more blocks are needed in a second stack to make 13?
	Recognize, write, and count the number **14**.	• Complete Practice Pages 253 and 254. • Challenge your child to draw a self-portrait that has 14 features to count: body parts, shoes, hat, buttons, jewelry, etc.
Bonus: Gross Motor Skills		• Write consonant letters and **short e** on paper circles and scatter them on the floor. Then, say a word such as **jet, pen, red,** or **leg**. Play some lively music. Can your child jump to each letter in the word?

Short Vowel Ee

Short Ee is the sound at the beginning of the word **eggs**. Color the pictures that begin with the **short Ee** sound.

Short Vowel Ee

Short Ee is the sound in the middle of the word **hen**. Help the hen get to the barn. Follow the path with the pictures whose names have the **short Ee** sound.

Short Vowel Ee

Say the name of each picture. Write the letter **e** to complete each word below.

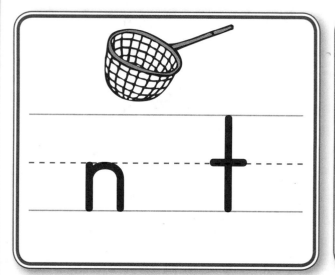

n t

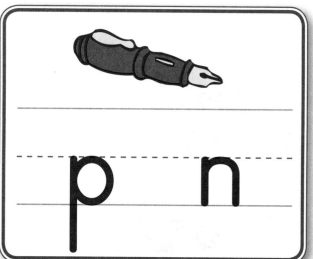

p n

b d

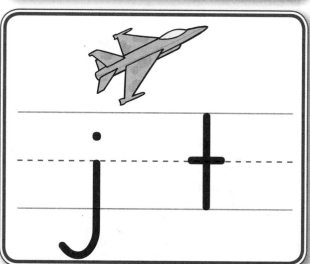

j t

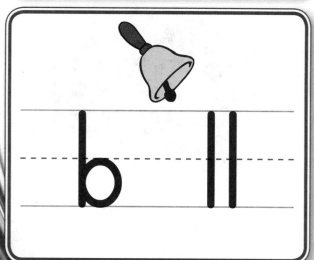

b ll

h n

Short Vowel Ee

Say the name of each picture. Write the letter **e** to complete each word below.

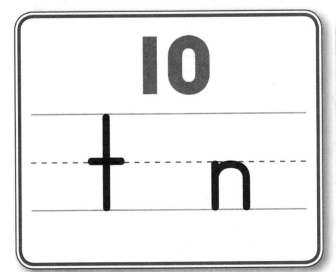
t _____ n

b _____ d

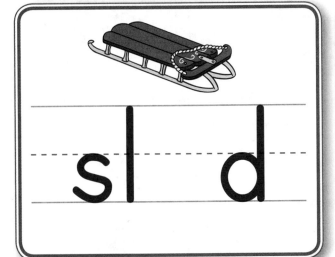
sl _____ d

f _____ nce

m _____ n

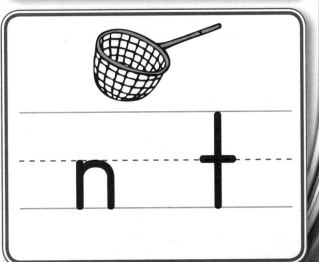
n _____ t

Short Vowel Ee

Read the words. Circle the picture that matches the word.

net

fence
 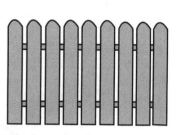

bell

ten
 **10**

Number 13

This is the number **13**. Color the picture.

How many things are in this picture? _____

Trace the 13s.

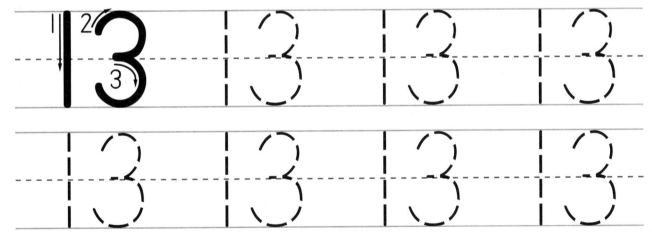

Write your own 13s.

_____

_____

13 Thirteen

Draw **13** doughnuts in the box.

Number 14

This is the number **14**. Color the picture.

How many things are in this picture? _____

Trace the 14s.

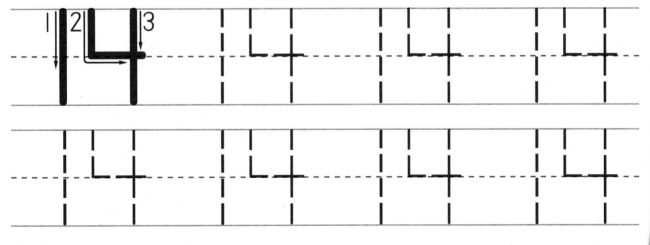

Write your own 14s.

_____

- -

_____

14 Fourteen

Connect the dots. Color the picture.

Week 24 Skills

Subject	Skill	Multi-Sensory Learning Activities
Reading and Language Arts	Identify the **short i** vowel sound.	• Complete Practice Pages 256–260. • Say these words: **sat**, **sit**, **fin**, **get**, **map**, **clip**, **men**. Have your child buzz like an insect when he or she hears the **short i** sound. • Say the nursery rhyme "Jack and Jill Went Up the Hill." Can your child identify the **short i** words in the rhyme?
Math	Recognize, write, and count the number **15**.	• Complete Practice Pages 261 and 262. • Ask your child to count 15 pennies or other small items. Can he or she put them into three equal groups and then count to 15 by fives?
	Recognize, write, and count the number **16**.	• Complete Practice Pages 263 and 264. • Write numbers **1–16** on colorful stickers or self-stick notes. Ask your child to arrange them on a sheet of paper in numerical order. Count to 16 together.
Bonus: Fine Motor Skills		• Fill several jars or clear drinking glasses with different numbers of candies. Make sure no jar has more than 16 pieces of candy. Then, have your child guess the number in each jar and record his or her guess. Let your child count the candies in each jar to see how close the guesses came!

Short Vowel Ii

Short Ii is the sound at the beginning of the word **igloo**. Color the pictures that begin with the **short Ii** sound.

Short Vowel Ii

Short Ii is the sound in the middle of the word **dish**. Say the name of each picture. Draw lines from the dish to the pictures with the **short Ii** sound.

Short Vowel Ii

Read the words. Draw a line from each word to the picture that matches it.

Short Vowel Ii

Short Ii is the sound you hear in the middle of the word **pig**. Say each picture name. Write **i** to complete each word below.

ch ___ ck

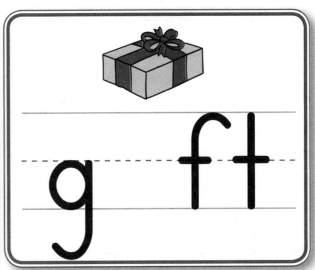

g ___ ft

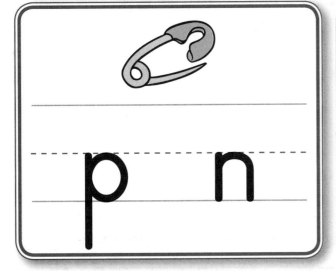

p ___ n

w ___ g

f ___ n

b ___ b

Short Vowel Ii

Say each picture name. Circle the word that names the picture. Write it on the line.

fin

tin

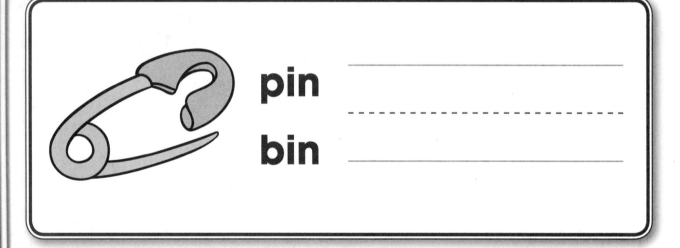

pin

bin

bin

fin

Number 15

This is the number **15**. Color the picture.

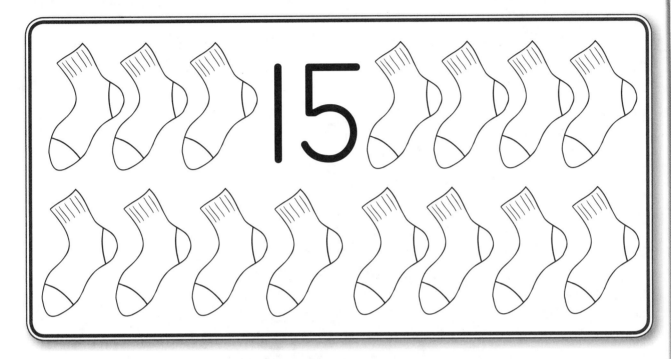

How many things are in this picture? _____

Trace the 15s.

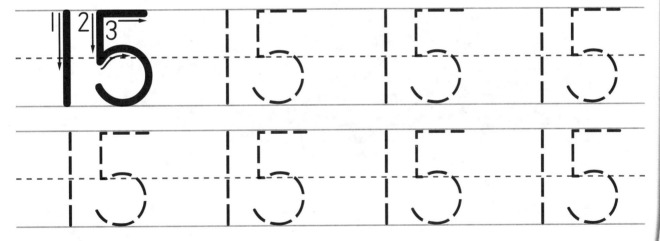

Write your own 15s.

_____

- - - - - - - - - - - - - - - - - - - -

_____

15 Fifteen

Write the missing pool ball numbers.

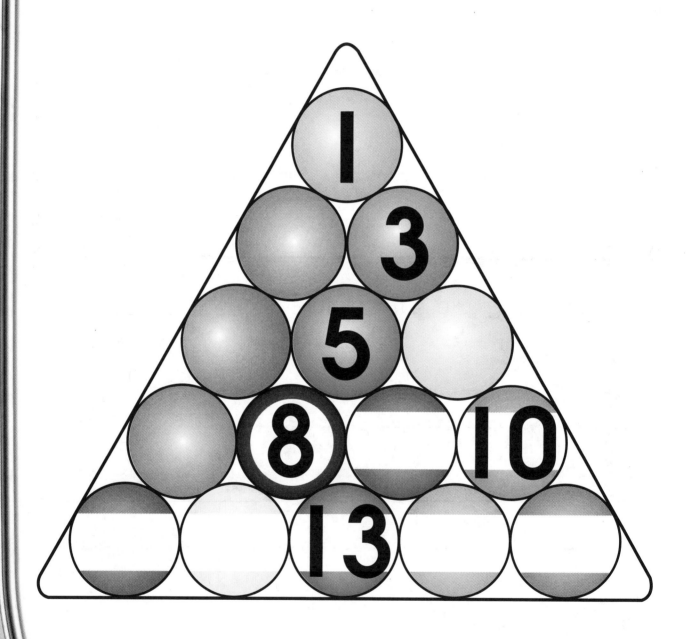

Number 16

This is the number **16**. Color the picture.

How many things are in this picture? _____

Trace the 16s.

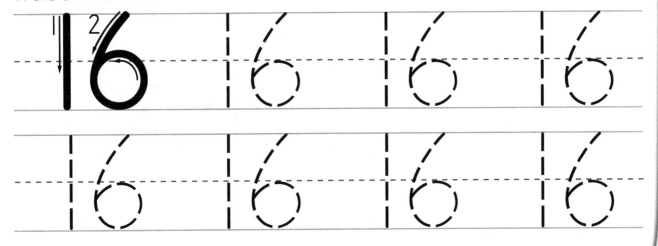

Write your own 16s.

_____

- -

_____

16 Sixteen

Draw eight legs on each spider.

How many legs are there in all? _____

Week 25 Skills

Subject	Skill	Multi-Sensory Learning Activities
Reading and Language Arts	Identify the **short o** vowel sound.	• Complete Practice Pages 266–270. • Read *Fox in Socks* or *Hop on Pop* by Dr. Seuss. As you read, ask your child to form an **o** shape with one hand each time he or she hears a word with **short o**. • Ask your child to join you in saying several words that contain **short o**, such as **job** and **stop**, emphasizing the vowel sound. Notice together how the open mouth drops and forms an **o**-like shape when making the sound.
Math	Recognize, write, and count the number **17**.	• Complete Practice Pages 271 and 272. • Make ten frames on two sheets of paper by dividing each sheet into two rows with five empty boxes in each row. Ask your child to fill the frames with pennies or other counters to show 17. Point out that one ten frame is full, while the other frame has seven full boxes.
	Recognize, write, and count the number **18**.	• Complete Practice Pages 273 and 274. • Use the ten frames created for the activity above. Ask your child to fill the boxes to show 18. Ask, "How many more would make 20? How many fewer would make 10?"
Bonus: Gross Motor Skills		• Design a short, indoor obstacle course for your child. Make sure to include actions that involve the **short o** words **on** and **off**. Time your child as he or she completes the course.

Short Vowel Oo

Short Oo is the sound at the beginning of the word **octopus**. Say each picture name. Color the socks that have the **short Oo** sound. Does this octopus have enough colored socks? _____

Short Vowel Oo

Look at the pictures. Color the pictures that begin with the **short Oo** sound.

Short Vowel Oo

Write the letter **o** to complete each word. Read the words. Then, find the pictures of the words at the bottom of the page and circle them.

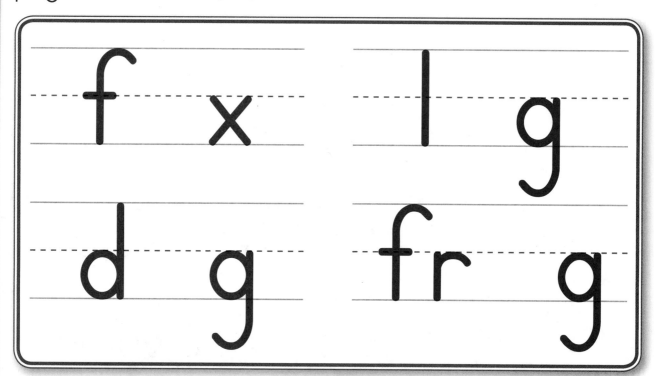

f _ x   l _ g

d _ g   fr _ g

Short Vowel Oo

Say each picture name. Write **o** to complete each word below.

r _ ck

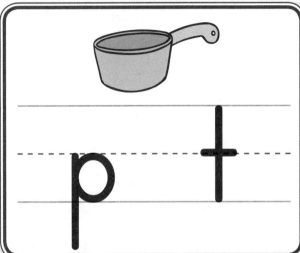

p _ t

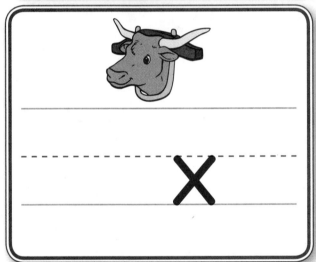

_ x

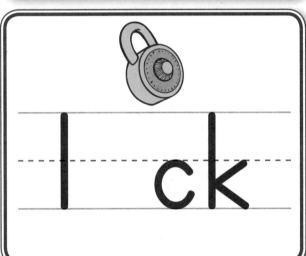

l _ ck

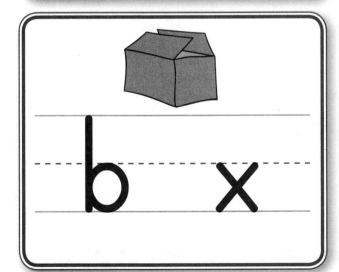

b _ x

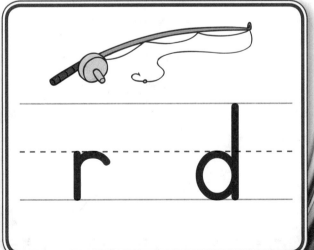

r _ d

Short Vowel Oo

Say each picture name. Say each word. Draw a line from each picture to the word that names the picture.

cot

tot

pot

COMPLETE YEAR KINDERGARTEN

Number 17

This is the number **17**. Color the picture.

How many things are in this picture? _____

Trace the 17s.

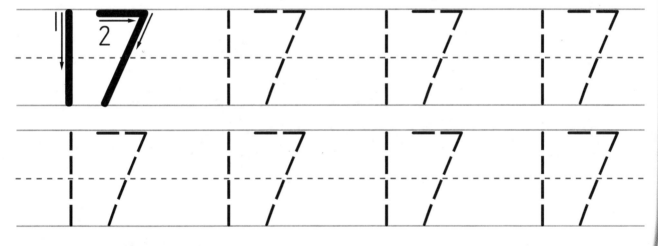

Write your own 17s.

_____

- -

_____

17 Seventeen

Circle each group of **17** things. Color the dog.

Number 18

This is the number **18**. Color the picture.

How many things are in this picture? _____

Trace the 18s.

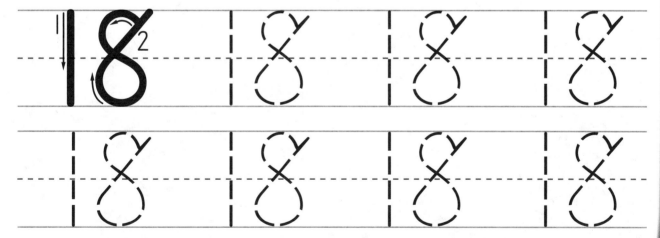

Write your own 18s.

_____

- -

_____

18 Eighteen

Help Filbert Fish find his way to the top. Write the numbers **1–18** in each bubble along the way.

Week 26 Skills

Subject	Skill	Multi-Sensory Learning Activities
Reading and Language Arts	Identify the **short u** vowel sound.	• Complete Practice Pages 276–280. • Read or tell the story "The Ugly Duckling." Ask your child to quack like a duck each time he or she hears a word with the **short u** sound. • Have your child stand on the bottom step of a stairway. Then, say a pair of words such as **sun** and **sand**. If your child correctly chooses the **short u** word, he or she can go up one step. Repeat with more pairs of words until your child reaches the top.
Math	Recognize, write, and count the number **19**.	• Complete Practice Pages 281 and 282. • Encourage your child to draw a night scene with a big moon and nine stars. Have him or her write numbers **1–10** on the moon and **11–19** on the stars.
	Recognize, write, and count the number **20**.	• Complete Practice Pages 283 and 284. • Hold up your ten fingers and ask your child to do the same. Lower one finger at a time as you count to 20 together.
Bonus: Fine Motor Skills		• Have your child use safe, rounded scissors to snip drinking straws into short segments. Then, he or she can thread the segments onto yarn and tie in circles to make napkin rings for a family meal.

Short Vowel Uu

Short Uu is the sound you hear in the middle of the word **bug**. Help the bug get to the leaf. Follow the path with the pictures whose names have the **short Uu** sound.

Short Vowel Uu

Short Uu is the sound you hear at the beginning of the word **umbrella**. Cut out the pictures at the bottom of the page. Say each picture name. If the picture has the **short Uu** sound, glue it on the umbrella.

Short Vowel Uu

Write the letter **u** to complete each word. Read the word. Draw a line to match each word with its picture.

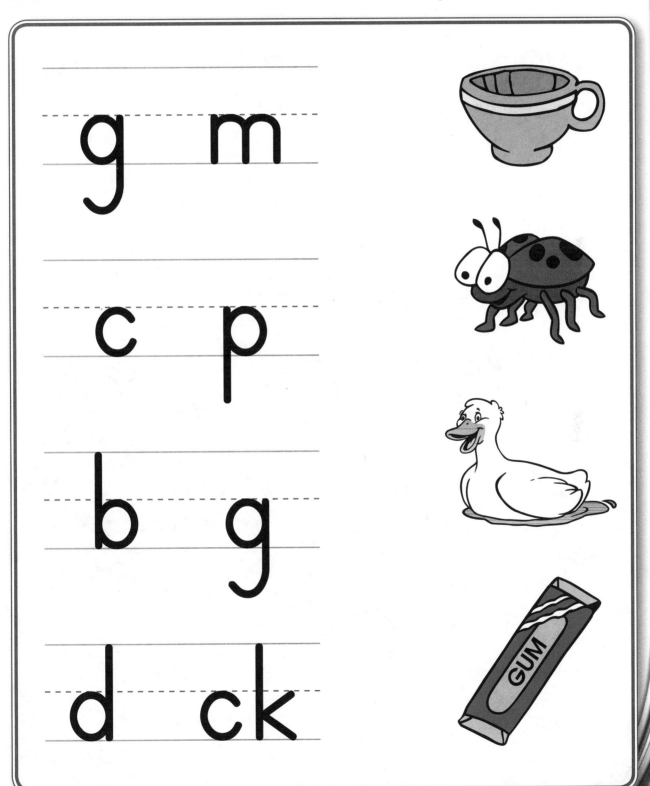

g __ m

c __ p

b __ g

d __ ck

Short Vowel Uu

Look at the pictures and read the words. Draw a line from each picture to the word that matches it.

cup   **bus**   **gum**   **mug**

Number 19

This is the number **19**. Color the picture.

How many things are in this picture? _____

Trace the 19s.

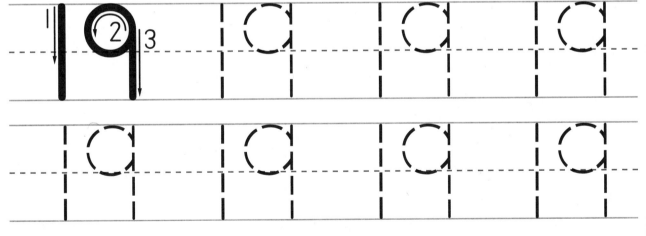

Write your own 19s.

_____

- -

_____

19 Nineteen

Draw **19** cookies in the cookie jar. Color the cookies. Number them from **1** to **19**.

Number 20

This is the number **20**. Color the picture.

How many things are in this picture? _____

Trace the 20s.

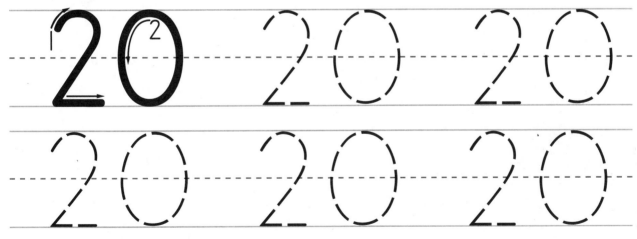

Write your own 20s.

_____

- -

_____

20 Twenty

Draw **20** freckles on the boy's face. Color the boy.

Week 27 Skills

Subject	Skill	Multi-Sensory Learning Activities
Reading and Language Arts	Review short vowel sounds.	• Complete Practice Pages 286–289. • Set these 10 objects on a tabletop: pan, pen, hat, cup, milk carton, slip of paper with **10** written on it, mop, sock, ring, picture of the sun. Can your child sort the objects according to their short vowel sounds? • Be silly and sing "Twinkle, Twinkle, Little Star" by substituting a short vowel sound for each word. Repeat with another short vowel sound.
Basic Skills	Understand the concepts **more** and **fewer**.	• Complete Practice Pages 291–294. • Play with two bowls and a supply of dry beans, pennies, or other small objects. Put some in each bowl and ask your child to tell which bowl has more and which has less. Your child may need to count to verify his or her answer. Let your child put items in the bowls for you to compare, too. • Say a number followed by "greater" or "less." Can your child quickly say a number that fits? Take turns, increasing speed until someone makes a mistake.
Bonus: Math		• Encourage your child to count by ones, fives, and tens while skipping or jumping rope. • Make up simple, real-world math problems for your child. For example, say, "If you have nine trucks and you get four more for your birthday, how many trucks do you have altogether?"

Vowel Sounds

Look at the picture in each box. Circle the pictures in that row that have the same vowel sound.

Vowel Sounds

Look at each picture. Draw a line to the letter that makes the same vowel sound.

Vowel Sounds

Look at each picture. Draw a line to the letter that makes the same vowel sound.

Vowel Sounds

Say each picture name. Cut out the words. Glue each word where it belongs.

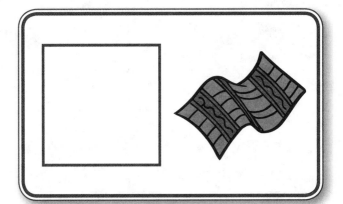

hat	pot	hen	fin	mat

More

Circle the group in each box that has more.

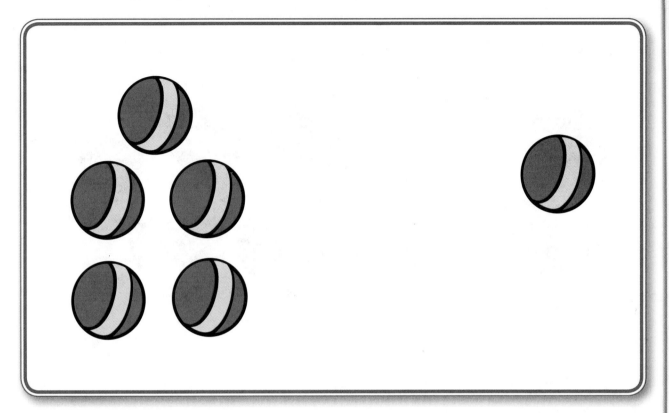

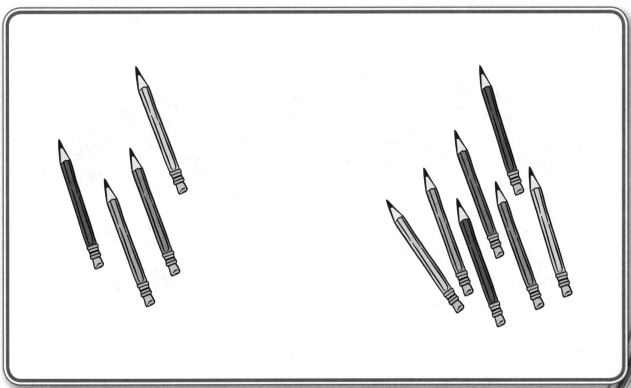

More

Circle the group in each box that has more.

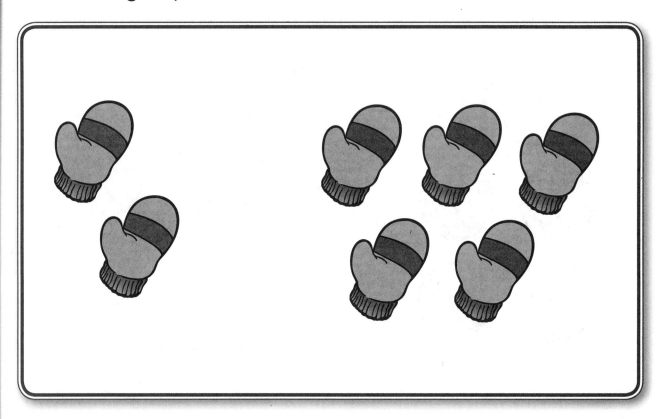

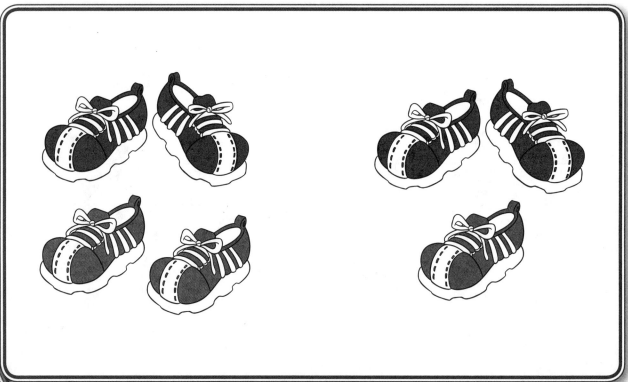

Fewer

Color the group in each box that has fewer.

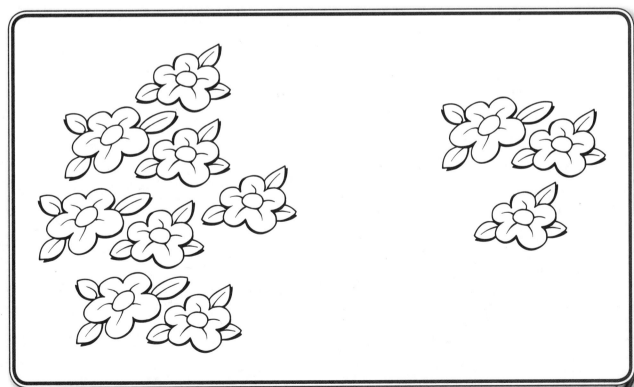

Fewer

Circle the group in each box that has fewer.

Third Quarter Check-Up

Basic Skills

❏ I can tell which group has more.

❏ I can tell which group has fewer.

Reading and Language Arts

❏ I know the sounds made by all 21 consonant letters.

❏ I can identify letters that spell sounds at the ends of words.

❏ I know the **short a** sound.

❏ I know the **short e** sound.

❏ I know the **short i** sound.

❏ I know the **short o** sound.

❏ I know the **short u** sound.

Math

❏ I recognize numbers **8–20**.

❏ I can write numbers **8–20**.

❏ I can count accurately to 20.

❏ I can compare two numbers and tell which is greater.

Final Project

Staple blank paper together to make a book with 20 pages. Write a large number **1–20** on each page. Then, find photos of yourself at each age from 1–5 and glue them on to illustrate the first few pages. For the other pages, draw pictures of what you might look like at that age. Write a word or sentence for each page.

Fourth Quarter Introduction

As the school year nears its end, many students are feeling confident about the new skills they have learned as kindergartners. This may be evident in more fluent handwriting, quick recognition of letters and sounds, and the ability to count and assign numbers accurately. As the days get warmer and children play outside in the evenings, don't forget to maintain school day routines and continue to support your child's academic growth at home.

Fourth Quarter Skills

Practice pages in this book for Weeks 28–36 will help your child improve the following skills.

Basic Skills
- Understand the concepts **more** and **fewer**
- Classify objects by category
- Sequence events
- Think critically in order to discriminate between similar objects and events

Reading and Language Arts
- Identify rhyming words
- Understand synonyms (words with similar meanings) and antonyms (words with opposite meanings)
- Recognize frequently-used words by sight
- Write sentences that begin with capital letters and end with punctuation marks
- Understand nouns and verbs
- Use capital letters to begin names
- Add **s** to make words plural
- Understand homophones, or words that sound alike but have different spellings and meanings
- Understand that word parts such as **–ful** and **–less** can be added to words to change their meanings

Math
- Work with ordinal numbers **first**, **second**, **third**, etc.
- Record counted objects on a graph
- Count to 100 by ones and tens
- Understand place value
- Add and subtract within 10

Multi-Sensory Learning Activities

Try these fun activities for enhancing your child's learning and development during the fourth quarter of the school year. Be sure to choose activities that include speaking, listening, touching, and active movement.

 Basic Skills

Provide one or more photos from each year of your child's life. Challenge your child to sequence the pictures in chronological order.

Talk about items in the produce section at the grocery store. Choose one item and ask your child whether it is a fruit or vegetable, whether it grows on a tree or in the ground, etc. Can your child find another food in the store that fits some of those same categories?

Reading and Language Arts

When you read aloud to your child, point out rhyming words and examine them together, noting that they often have the same ending letters.

Encourage your child to draw a picture to send to a relative or friend. It should include one or more sentences that tell a story about the picture. Show how to begin each sentence with a capital letter and end it with a punctuation mark. Help your child address the envelope for mailing the picture, making sure to begin names with capital letters.

Help your child use index cards to make flash cards for words that he or she knows how to read. Include familiar sight words such as **the, it**, and **and**; familiar nouns such as **boy, cat**, and **school**; familiar verbs such as **run, play**, and **go**; and words that are meaningful to your child, such as the names of friends, pets, and activities.

 Math

Recall your child's length at birth and cut a piece of string or yarn to match. Ask, "How much have you grown? How many "baby lengths" does it take to equal your current height?"

Use this rhyme to practice counting by tens: 10, 20, 30, 40/Count by tens when you're in a hurry/50, 60, 70, 80/Quicker than ones, little matey/90, 100, we did it/We did it/We counted to 100 in less than a minute!

Fourth Quarter Introduction, cont.

Look for a line of ants outside. Can your child tell which ant is first, second, etc.?

Add and subtract while doing everyday activities with your child. Add the number of toys on two shelves or the number of dogs in two areas of a park. Subtract to find the number of days left in the week.

 **Fine Motor Skills**

Buy inexpensive cut flowers and some greenery. Alternately, go for a walk and pick some dandelions and wildflowers. Allow your child to arrange the flowers in a vase to make a spring centerpiece.

 **Gross Motor Skills**

Have fun with your child performing the actions described in this poem.

I wiggle my thumbs and clap my hands,
And then I stomp my feet.
I turn to the left, I turn to the right,
And make my fingers meet.

I raise them high and let them down,
I give another clap.
I wave my hands and fold my hands,
And put them in my lap.

 **Seasonal Fun**

Take a walk outside and use all your senses to experience the spring season. Feel new grass. Smell overturned dirt. Listen to a rushing creek or river. Look for birds and earthworms.

Read *And Then It's Spring* by Julie Fogliano. After reading, have your child use the pictures to retell the story.

Week 28 Skills

Subject	Skill	Multi-Sensory Learning Activities
Reading and Language Arts	Recognize rhyming words.	• Complete Practice Pages 300–304. • Find rhyming words in nursery rhymes, songs, and hand-clapping games. Substitute other words that rhyme. For example, in "Rub a Dub Dub, Three Men in a Tub," what other words could take the place of **tub**? Encourage your child to supply real words such as **sub** as well as silly, made-up words such as **fub**.
Basic Skills	Understand the concepts **more** and **fewer**.	• Complete Practice Pages 305–308. • Let your child fill two clear plastic containers with different amounts of water. Which container has more water? Which has less? Add water or pour some out. Now which has more?
Bonus: Math		• Choose five objects such as a rock, a sponge, a scrap of paper, an eraser, and an apple. Ask your child to predict which objects will float. Then, let your child test each in a bucket of water. Help him or her make a simple chart to show the results.
Bonus: Fine Motor Skills		• Let your child make an edible insect. Spread cream cheese between two round crackers. Place three pretzel sticks in each side. Use dabs of cream cheese to attach raisin "eyes."

Rhyming Pictures

Look at the pictures below. Draw lines to match the rhyming pictures.

Rhyming Pictures

Look at the pictures below. Draw lines to match the rhyming pictures.

Rhyming Pairs

Words that have the same ending sounds are called rhyming words. Circle the pairs that rhyme.

map   nest

dog   frog

hat   bat

kite   mop

can   fan

rat   pig

Rhyming Pairs

Look at each pair of words and pictures. Circle the pairs that rhyme.

nose   hose

beet   feet

star   jar

box   fox

dish   fish

cake   cap

Rhyming Pairs

Think of a word that rhymes with each picture. Draw a picture. Write the word.

bug

frog

More and Fewer

Count the blocks each child is playing with. Circle the child who has more blocks.

More and Fewer

Count the blocks in each group. Circle the group of blocks that has more.

More and Fewer

Count the blocks in the first box. Then, draw a group of blocks that has more.

More and Fewer

Count the cars each child is playing with. Circle the child who has fewer cars.

Week 29 Skills

Subject	Skill	Multi-Sensory Learning Activities
Basic Skills	Classify objects by category.	• Complete Practice Pages 310–313. • Let your child sort a deck of cards according to suit. How else could the cards be sorted? • Gather toy vehicles or pictures of trains, boats, planes, etc. How many ways can your child sort them into different categories?
Math	Work with ordinal numbers.	• Complete Practice Pages 314–318. • At bedtime, tell your child what you did today. Model using ordinal numbers by saying, "First, I…. Second, I…," etc. Encourage your child to use ordinal numbers to tell you about his or her day. • When standing in line at the store, ask your child to point out the first person in line, the second person in line, etc.
Bonus: Reading and Language Arts		• Help your child recognize how many words he or she already knows how to read. When reading aloud, have your child point out familiar words. Don't forget small words such as **a** and **the**. Try to make a list of 100 words your child can read!
Bonus: Gross Motor Skills		• Have fun playing sidewalk hockey with your child using two brooms, a lid or other plastic disk, and goals marked with sidewalk chalk.

Classifying: These Keep Me Warm

Color the things that keep you warm.

socks

apple

earmuffs

lunch box

cookie

coat

umbrella

hat

gloves

book

COMPLETE YEAR KINDERGARTEN

Classifying: Objects

Help Dan clean up the park. Circle the litter. Underline the coins. Draw a box around the balls.

Home You Go!

Help the animals get home! Draw a line from each animal to its home.

What Goes Together?

Draw a line to match the things that go together.

First

Circle the first thing in each row.

Second

Circle the second thing in each row.

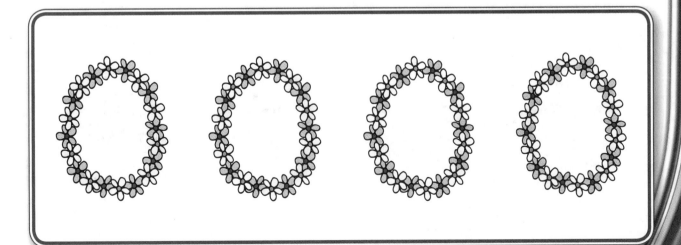

Third

Circle the third thing in each row.

COMPLETE YEAR KINDERGARTEN

Last

Circle the last thing in each row.

Ordinal Numbers

Color the first leaf red. Circle the third leaf.

Color the fourth balloon purple. Draw a line under the second balloon.

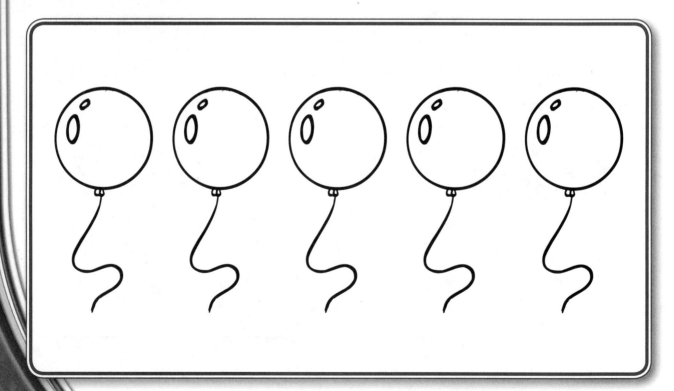

Week 30 Skills

Subject	Skill	Multi-Sensory Learning Activities
Basic Skills	Sequence events.	• Complete Practice Pages 320–323. • Talk about ways your family has changed over time. Recall family additions, pets, moves, and other milestones. Ask your child to create and illustrate a family time line. • Look at a calendar with your child. Talk about each month, what the weather is like during that time, and whether it contains holidays or birthdays. Similarly, talk about what happens during each day of the week.
Math	Count objects and use a graph to show the data.	• Complete Practice Pages 325–327. • Let your child help you unload silverware from the dishwasher. Ask him or her to sort forks, spoons, etc. and count the number of each. Create a simple graph to show the information.
	Think about measurable attributes such as height and weight.	• Complete Practice Page 328. • Cut three lengths of yarn. Have your child put them in order from shortest to longest. Then, have your child put three toys or kitchen utensils in size order.
Bonus: Fine Motor Skills		• Plant grass seed in a foam cup. Water the seeds gently and place the cup in a sunny window. Draw a face on the cup with markers. Soon, the character will have green hair!

January

Sunday	Monday	Tuesday	Wednesday	Thursday	Friday	Saturday
			1	2	3	4
5	6	7	8	9	10	11
12	13	14	15	16	17	18
19	20	21	22	23	24	25
26	27	28	29	30	31	

What Comes First?

Circle the picture in each row that shows what happened first. Color the pictures.

What Comes Last?

Circle the picture in each row that shows what happened last. Color the pictures.

Ducky Destination

Help Ducky have a great vacation. Number the pictures **1**, **2**, **3**, and **4** to show the correct order.

What Comes First?

Color the pictures. Cut out the pictures in each row and put them in order to show what comes first, second, and third.

Graphing

Count the pets in the window. Then, color one box for each animal on the graph below.

6				
5				
4				
3				
2				
1				

Graphing

Count the shapes in the picture. Then, complete the graph below.

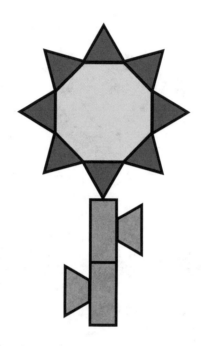

8				
7				
6				
5				
4				
3				
2				
1				

Graphing

Look at the graph on page 326. Then, answer the questions below.

- How many triangles are there? _____

- How many rectangles are there? _____

- How many octagons are there? _____

- How many trapezoids are there? _____

- Which two shapes are there the same number of?

  _____ and _____

- How many shapes are there all together? _____

Watch Me Grow

I am growing each day!

_____

- -

I am _____ inches tall.

_____

- -

I weigh _____ pounds.

Week 31 Skills

Subject	Skill	Multi-Sensory Learning Activities
Reading and Language Arts	Recognize antonyms (words with opposite meanings).	• Complete Practice Pages 330–333. • When talking and reading with your child, substitute opposite words to make silly sentences. For example, say, "Help me get something from that low shelf." Let your child correct you, giving the antonym (**high**) that is needed in the sentence.
	Recognize synonyms (words with similar meanings).	• Complete Practice Page 334. • Invite your child to act out these words with very similar meanings: **cool/chilly/freezing**, **touch/grab/snatch**, **look/stare/glance**.
Math	Count to 100 by ones and tens.	• Complete Practice Pages 335–337. • Help your child make a poster that shows 100 things. It could have 100 stickers, 100 thumbprints, or 100 candy wrappers. Encourage your child to arrange the objects in groups of 10. Use the poster to practice counting by ones and tens.
	Understand place value.	• Complete Practice Page 338. • Make a stack of 10 interlocking blocks. Ask your child to stack single blocks beside it to represent numbers such as **12**, **16**, and **18**.
Bonus: Gross Motor Skills		• Do exercises with your child such as jumping jacks, sit-ups, and leg lifts. Then, help your child find his or her pulse and count the number of beats per minute.

10 20 30 40 50

Opposites

Opposites are things that are different in every way. Draw a line to match the opposites.

day

little

front

sad

happy

night

big

back

COMPLETE YEAR KINDERGARTEN

Opposites

Draw a line to match the opposites.

old

girl

boy

full

open

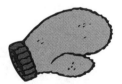

new

empty

closed

Opposites

Draw a picture of the opposite.

day

night

sad

happy

Antonyms

Antonyms are words that mean the opposite of another word.

Examples: **hot** and **cold**
            short and **tall**

Draw a line from each word on the left to its antonym on the right.

sad	**white**
bottom	**stop**
black	**fat**
tall	**top**
thin	**hard**
little	**found**
cold	**short**
lost	**hot**
go	**big**
soft	**happy**

Synonyms

Read each sentence. Fill in the blanks with the synonyms.

friend	tired	story	presents	little

 I want to go to bed because I am very <u>sleepy</u>.

_____

 On my birthday I like to open my <u>gifts</u>.

_____

 My <u>pal</u> and I like to play together.

_____

 My favorite <u>tale</u> is *Cinderella*.

_____

 The mouse was so <u>tiny</u> that it was hard to catch him.

_____

Counting

Write the missing numbers.

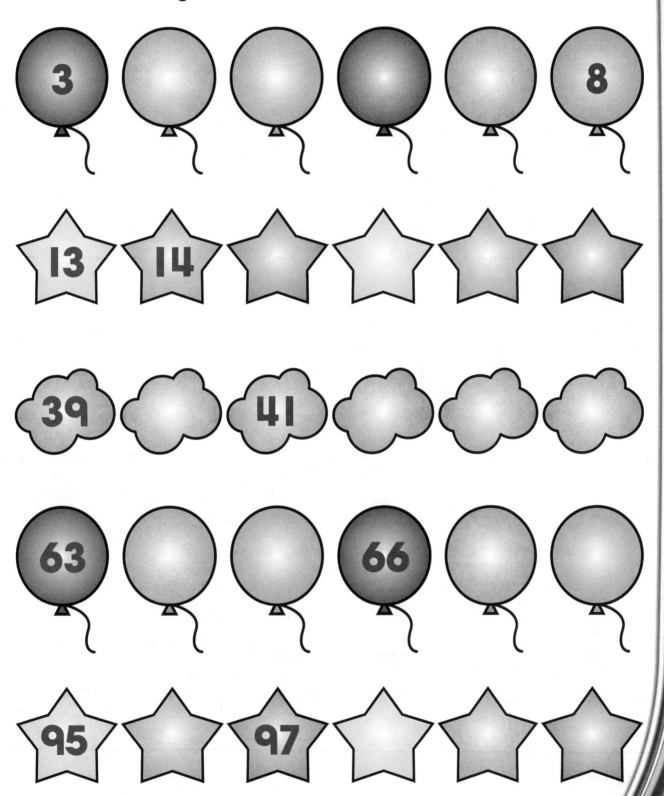

3					8
13	14				
39		41			
63			66		
95		97			

Counting by 1s and 10s

Write the missing numbers.

Count by 1s.

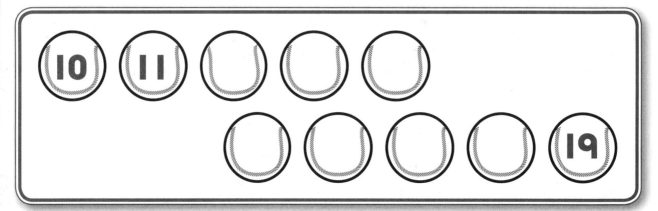

Count by 10s.

Count by 10s.

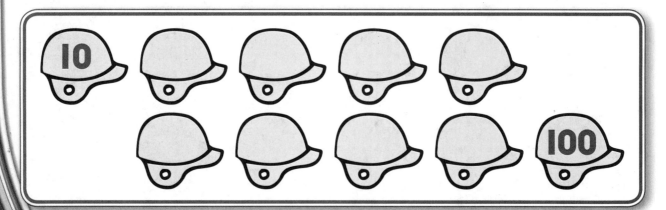

Counting by 10s

Connect the dots from **10** to **100** to find a circus treat.
Then, color the picture.

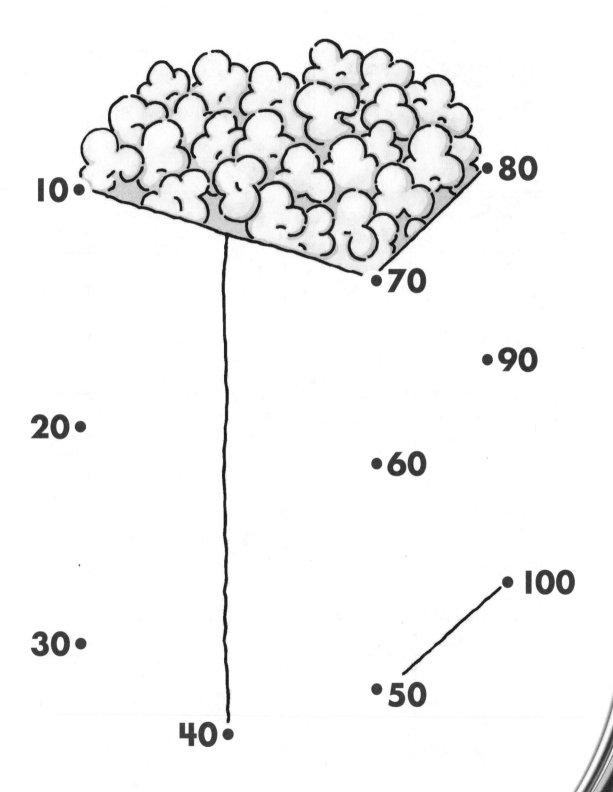

Table Time

Draw cubes in the tens and ones columns to show the numbers. The first one is done for you.

	tens	ones
11	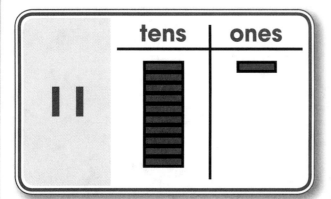	

	tens	ones
15		

	tens	ones
12		

	tens	ones
16		

	tens	ones
13		

	tens	ones
17		

	tens	ones
14		

	tens	ones
18		

Week 32 Skills

Subject	Skill	Multi-Sensory Learning Activities
Reading and Language Arts	Recognize frequently-used words.	• Complete Practice Pages 340–344. • Refer to the list of Kindergarten Sight Words on page 394. How many of these words does your child know? How many can he or she find in a favorite picture book? • Invite your child to spell words with magnetic letters on the refrigerator or on a cookie sheet. Include sight words such as **that** and **on**. Use your phone or another device to take a picture of each completed word. Compile the pictures into a slide show for your child to review.
Math	Add within 5.	• Complete Practice Pages 345–348. • Create simple story problems related to your child's interests. For example, say, "Three friends were playing soccer. Two more wanted to play. How many were playing altogether?" • Practice adding with candies, crackers, veggie sticks, and other items around the house.
Bonus: Fine Motor Skills		• Draw large outlines of numbers **1–5** and symbols **+** and **=** on blank paper. Ask your child to cut them out with rounded safety scissors, color them, and use them to assemble addition sentences.

Word Recognition: Things

Draw a line to match each word with its picture.

cat

flower

car

tree

Word Recognition: Things

Draw a line to match each word with its picture.

ball

apple

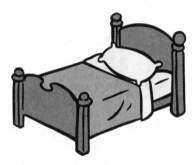

bed

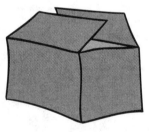

box

Word Recognition: Descriptions

Draw a line to match each word with its picture.

tall

short

old

big

Word Recognition: Descriptions

Draw a line to match each word with its picture.

little

happy

sad

funny

Word Recognition: Colors

Color each picture the correct color.

red shirt

yellow ball

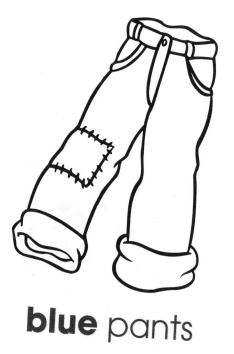

blue pants

green car

Addition 1, 2

Addition means "putting together" or adding two or more numbers to find the sum. **+** is a plus sign. It means to add the numbers. **=** is an equal sign. It tells how much they are together.

Count the cats and tell how many.

Addition

Count the shapes and write the numbers below to tell how many in all.

_____   _____   _____

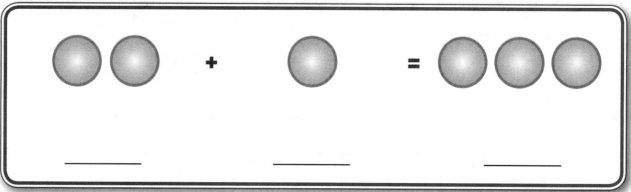

_____   _____   _____

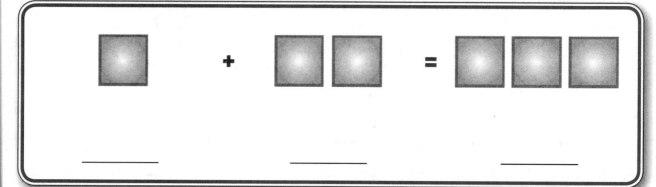

_____   _____   _____

_____   _____   _____

Addition 1–5

Look at the red numbers and draw that many more flowers in the pot. Count them to get your total.

Example: 3 + 2 = ___5___

1 + 4 = _____

$$\begin{array}{r} 1 \\ +\ 1 \\ \hline \end{array}$$

$$\begin{array}{r} 2 \\ +\ 2 \\ \hline \end{array}$$

3 + 1 = _____

Addition 1–5

Add the numbers. Put your answers in the nests.

Example: 2 + 3 =

1 + 2 =

1 + 3 =

4 + 1 =

1 + 1 =

Week 33 Skills

Subject	Skill	Multi-Sensory Learning Activities
Reading and Language Arts	Recognize frequently-used words.	• Complete Practice Pages 350–353. • Use a free Web site to create word search puzzles that include words your child is learning to read. Include sight words such as **he**, **she**, and **it**. Completing the puzzles is a great way for your child to practice. • Show your child how to make word pyramids to practice spelling new words. For the word **walk**, write **w** on the first line, **wa** on the second line, **wal** on the third line, and **walk** on the fourth line.
Math	Add within 10.	• Complete Practice Pages 355–358. • Play with 10 craft sticks and two cups. Put several sticks in each cup. Can your child quickly add the two numbers and give the sum? • Read *Domino Addition* by Lynette Long. Ask your child to solve several addition problems from the book. Make addition problems with your own dominoes, too.
Bonus: Gross Motor Skills		• Use sidewalk chalk to make a hopscotch board outside. Show your child how to play the basic game with numbers written inside the squares. Alternately, write letters, words, or addition problems inside the squares to practice reading and math skills.

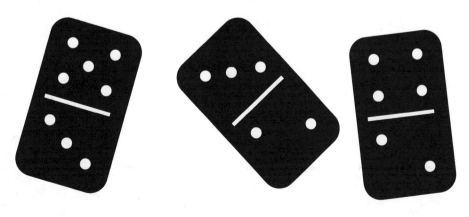

Word Recognition: People

Draw a line to match each word with its picture.

boy

girl

man

woman

Word Recognition: Action Words

Draw a line to match the action word with the person doing that action.

walk

run

talk

eat

Word Recognition: Action Words

Draw a line to match the action word with the person doing that action.

play

ride

sit

cook

Fruit and Vegetable Puzzles

Color and cut out the puzzle pieces below. Match each picture with its name.

apple

carrot

pumpkin

grapes

Addition

Draw the correct number of dots next to the numbers in each problem. Add up the number of dots to find your answers.

Example:

$$3 + 2 = 5$$

$$2 + 2 = 4$$

$$4 + 2$$

$$1 + 5 = \underline{}$$

$$3 + 1$$

$$4 + 3 = \underline{}$$

$$6 + 2$$

$$5 + 3 = \underline{}$$

Addition 6–10

Add the numbers. Put your answers in the doghouses.

Example: 4 + 2 =  6

2 + 6 =

7 + 3 =

6 + 1 =

4 + 5 =

6 + 2 =

7 + 2 =

Picture Problems: Addition

Solve the number problem under each picture.

6 + 2 = _____

4 + 4 = _____

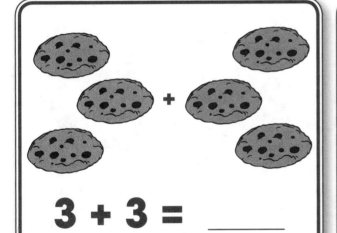

3 + 3 = _____

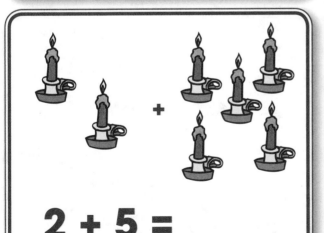

2 + 5 = _____

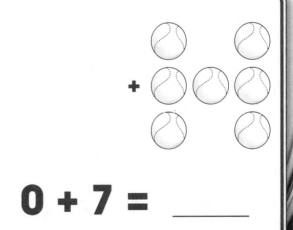

1 + 5 = _____

0 + 7 = _____

Picture Problems: Addition

Use the pictures to fill in the missing numbers.

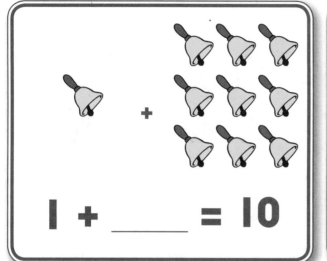

1 + _____ = 10

2 + _____ = 10

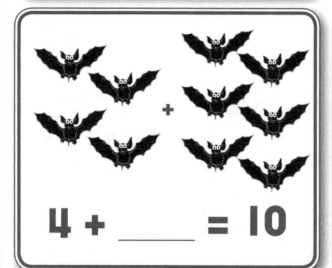

4 + _____ = 10

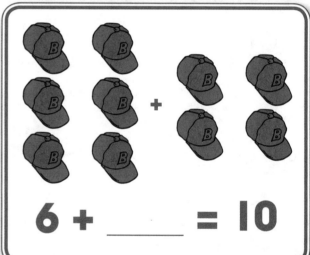

6 + _____ = 10

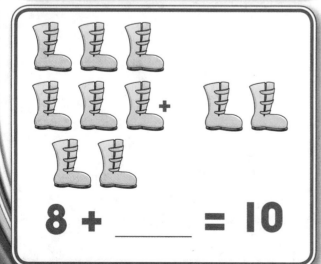

8 + _____ = 10

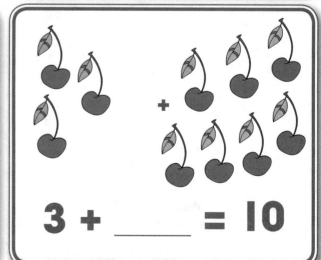

3 + _____ = 10

Week 34 Skills

Subject	Skill	Multi-Sensory Learning Activities
Reading and Language Arts	Write sentences that begin with capital letters and end with punctuation marks.	• Complete Practice Pages 360–363. • Invite your child to examine each sentence in a picture book. Does it begin with a capital letter? Does it end with a punctuation mark? How many times are **?** and **!** used? • Write several sentences on blank paper. Then, cut apart the words and the final punctuation mark. Can your child re-assemble the sentences, making sure that each begins with a capital letter and ends with a punctuation mark?
Math	Subtract within 10.	• Complete Practice Pages 364–368. • Make sure your child understands subtraction, or "taking away." Make a ten frame by dividing a blank sheet of paper into two rows with five boxes in each row. Fill the boxes with pennies or other small counters. Then, take one or more counters away. Can your child tell how many are left?
Bonus: Fine Motor Skills		• Divide sheets of construction paper into columns. Have your child use rounded safety scissors to cut on the lines to form long strips. Then, have him or her snip each strip into a number of small squares. The colored squares may be glued onto a background to make a mosaic.

Statements

Statements are sentences that tell us something. They begin with a capital letter and end with a period.

Write the sentences on the lines below. Begin each sentence with a capital letter and end it with a period.

1. we like to ride our bikes

   _____

2. we go down the hill very fast

   _____

3. we keep our bikes shiny and clean

   _____

4. we know how to change the tires

   _____

Surprising Sentences

Surprising sentences tell a strong feeling and end with an exclamation point. A surprising sentence may be only one or two words showing fear, surprise, or pain.
Example: Oh, no!

Put a period at the end of the sentences that tell something. Put an exclamation point at the end of the sentences that tell a strong feeling. Put a question mark at the end of the sentences that ask a question.

1. The cheetah can run very fast

2. Wow

3. Look at that cheetah go

4. Can you run fast

5. Oh, my

6. You're faster than I am

7. Let's run together

8. We can run as fast as a cheetah

9. What fun

10. Do you think cheetahs get tired

Commands

Commands tell someone to do something. **Example:** "Be careful." It can also be written as "Be careful!" if it tells a strong feeling.

Put a period at the end of the command sentences. Use an exclamation point if the sentence tells a strong feeling. Write your own commands on the lines below.

1. Clean your room

2. Now

3. Be careful with your goldfish

4. Watch out

5. Be a little more careful

_____

_____

Questions

Questions are sentences that ask something. They begin with a capital letter and end with a question mark.

Write the questions on the lines below. Begin each sentence with a capital letter and end it with a question mark.

1. will you be my friend

   _____

2. what is your name

   _____

3. are you eight years old

   _____

4. do you like rainbows

   _____

Subtraction 1–5

Subtract the red numbers by crossing out that many flowers in the pot. Count the ones not crossed out to get the total.

Example: 2 – 1 = __1__

5 – 2 = _____

$$\begin{array}{r} 4 \\ -\ 2 \\ \hline \end{array}$$

$$\begin{array}{r} 3 \\ -\ 1 \\ \hline \end{array}$$

4 – 3 = _____

Subtraction 1–5

Count the fruit in each bowl. Write your answers on the blanks. Circle the problem that matches your answer.

$$\begin{array}{r} 5 \\ -1 \\ \hline \end{array}$$
$$\begin{array}{r} 4 \\ -2 \\ \hline \end{array}$$

$$4$$

$$\begin{array}{r} 3 \\ -0 \\ \hline \end{array}$$
$$\begin{array}{r} 4 \\ -2 \\ \hline \end{array}$$

___

$$\begin{array}{r} 5 \\ -1 \\ \hline \end{array}$$
$$\begin{array}{r} 4 \\ -3 \\ \hline \end{array}$$

___

$$\begin{array}{r} 3 \\ -2 \\ \hline \end{array}$$
$$\begin{array}{r} 5 \\ -0 \\ \hline \end{array}$$

___

Subtraction

Draw the correct number of dots next to the numbers in each problem. Cross out the ones subtracted to find your answer.

Example:

$$\begin{array}{r} 5 \\ -2 \\ \hline 3 \end{array}$$ ● ● ● ✗✗

$2 - 1 = \underline{1}$ ● ✗

$$\begin{array}{r} 8 \\ -6 \\ \hline \end{array}$$

$4 - 2 = \underline{}$

$$\begin{array}{r} 6 \\ -1 \\ \hline \end{array}$$

$3 - 1 = \underline{}$

$$\begin{array}{r} 4 \\ -3 \\ \hline \end{array}$$

$9 - 6 = \underline{}$

Picture Problems: Subtraction

Solve the number problem under each picture.

5 - 2 = _____

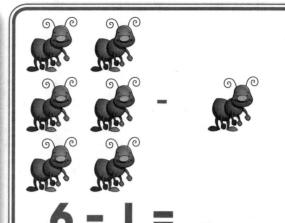

6 - 1 = _____

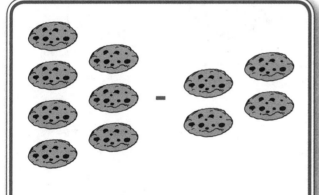

7 - 4 = _____

8 - 3 = _____

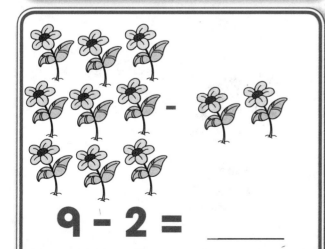

9 - 2 = _____

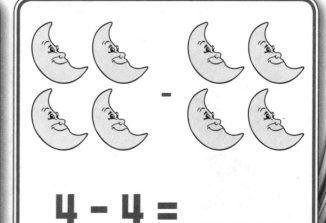

4 - 4 = _____

Subtraction 6–10

Count the flowers. Write your answer on the blank. Circle the problem that matches your answer.

$$10 \atop -1$$ $$9 \atop -1$$

_____

$$7 \atop -2$$ $$9 \atop -3$$

_____

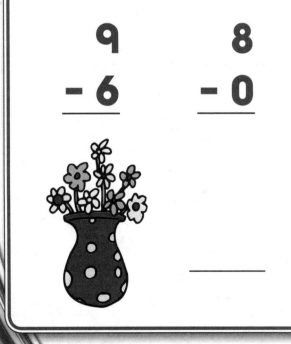

$$9 \atop -6$$ $$8 \atop -0$$

_____

$$10 \atop -2$$ $$8 \atop -1$$

_____

Week 35 Skills

Subject	Skill	Multi-Sensory Learning Activities
Reading and Language Arts	Understand that nouns are naming words.	• Complete Practice Pages 370 and 371. • Use index cards to make labels for things and places at your house. They should have nouns such as **door**, **mirror**, **kitchen**, **book**, and **plant**. Tape the labels to the items. Remind your child that nouns name people, places, and things.
	Understand that verbs are action words.	• Complete Practice Pages 372 and 373. • Play "Verb Charades" with your child. Act out familiar verbs such as **run**, **reach**, **clap**, or **smile**. Take turns guessing. Remind your child that verbs are action words.
Math	Practice addition and subtraction.	• Complete Practice Pages 374–378. • Provide a pile of pennies for your child to add and subtract. Write the symbols **+**, **-**, and **=** on self-sticking notes and encourage your child to use them with the pennies to create addition and subtraction equations.
Bonus: Gross Motor Skills		• Help your child bend craft wire or old hangers into bubble wands with different shapes. Use the wands with a solution made from equal parts dish detergent and corn syrup mixed with water. Do the different wands make bubbles with different shapes?

Nouns

A **noun** is the name of a person, place, or thing.

Read the story and circle all the nouns. Then, write the nouns next to the pictures below.

1. Our family likes to go to the park.

_____   _____

2. We play on the swings.

_____

3. We eat cake.

_____

4. We drink lemonade.

_____

5. We throw the ball to our dog.

_____   _____

6. Then we go home.

_____

Nouns

Look through a magazine. Cut out pictures of nouns and glue them below. Write the name of the noun next to the picture.

NOUNS

Verbs

A **verb** is the action word in a sentence. Verbs tell what something does or that something exists.

Example: Run, **sleep**, and **jump** are verbs.

Circle the verbs in the sentences below.

1. We play baseball every day.

2. Susan pitches the ball very well.

3. Mike swings the bat harder than anyone.

4. Chris slides into home base.

5. Laura hit a home run.

Verbs

Verbs are words that tell what a person or a thing can do.

Example: The girl pats the dog.
The word **pats** is the verb. It shows action.

Draw a line between the verbs and the pictures that show the action.

eat

run

sleep

swim

sing

hop

Picture Problems: Subtraction

Solve the number problem under each picture.

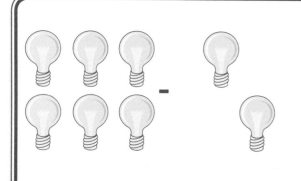

6 - 2 = _____

9 - 5 = _____

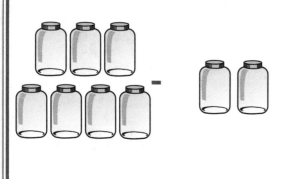

7 - 2 = _____

4 - 1 = _____

8 - 1 = _____

4 - 0 = _____

Picture Problems: Addition and Subtraction

Solve the number problem under each picture.

7 − 4 = _____

1 + 4 = _____

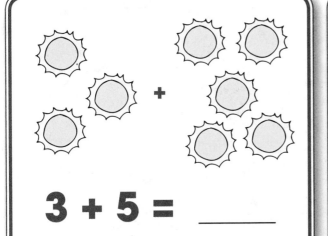

3 + 5 = _____

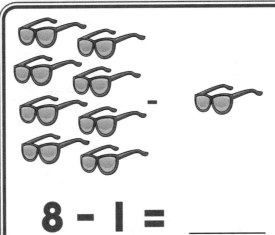

8 − 1 = _____

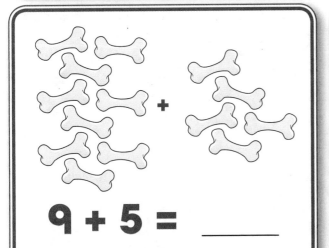

9 + 5 = _____

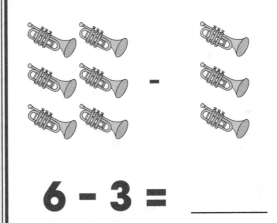

6 − 3 = _____

Picture Problems: Addition and Subtraction

Solve the number problem under each picture. Write **+** or **–** to show if you should add or subtract.

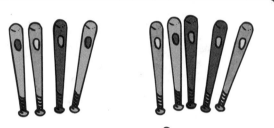

How many s in all?

4 + 5 = _____

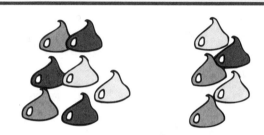

How many s in all?

7   5 = _____

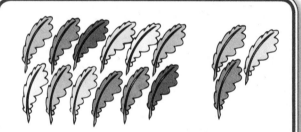

How many s are left?

12   3 = _____

How many s are left?

15   8 = _____

How many s in all?

5   8 = _____

How many s are left?

11   4 = _____

Picture Problems: Addition and Subtraction

Solve the number problem under each picture. Write **+** or **−** to show if you should add or subtract.

How many s in all?

7 + 5 = _____

How many s are left?

8   3 = _____

How many s are left?

9   4 = _____

How many s in all?

14   1 = _____

How many s are left?

15   6 = _____

How many s in all?

9   5 = _____

Review: Addition and Subtraction

Solve the number problem under each picture. Write **+** or **–** to show if you should add or subtract.

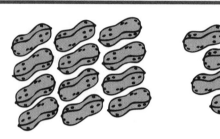

How many s are left?

12   4 = _____

How many s in all?

6   8 = _____

How many s are left?

4   4 = _____

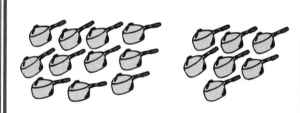

How many s are left?

11   7 = _____

How many s in all?

9   3 = _____

How many s in all?

10   0 = _____

Week 36 Skills

Subject	Skill	Multi-Sensory Learning Activities
Reading and Language Arts	Begin names with a capital letter.	• Complete Practice Page 380. • Ask your child to draw a family portrait. Encourage him or her to label each person with his or her name, making sure to begin each name with a capital letter.
	Add **s** to make words plural.	• Complete Practice Pages 381 and 382. • Wrap two fuzzy pipe cleaners around the end of a pencil and affix wiggle eyes to each to make a snakes pointer. When you read together, ask your child to use it to point out words that mean "more than one" and end with **s**.
	Understand homophones, or words that sound alike but have different spellings and meanings.	• Complete Practice Page 383. • Read *Dear Deer* by Gene Barretta or *The King Who Rained* by Fred Gwynne. These fun and silly books are all about homophones.
	Understand that word parts such as **–ful** and **–less** can be added to words to change their meanings.	• Complete Practice Page 384. • Make word-part addition problems. For example, **un + happy = unhappy**.
Basic Skills	Think critically in order to discriminate between similar objects and events.	• Complete Practice Pages 385–388. • Play "20 Questions." Think of an object and invite your child to ask up to 20 questions that require a "yes" or "no" answer in order to guess the item. Model how to narrow the possibilities. For example, a first question might be, "Is it bigger than me?"

Yes? No?

Names

You are a special person. Your name begins with a capital letter. We put a capital letter at the beginning of people's names because they are special. Write your name. Did you remember to use a capital letter?

_____

- -

_____

Write each person's name. Use a capital letter at the beginning.

Ted _____

Katie _____

Mike _____

Tim _____

More Than One

An **s** at the end of a word often means there is more than one. Look at each picture. Circle the correct word. Write the word on the line.

two

dog   dogs

one

bikes   bike

three

toys   toy

two

cat   cats

More Than One

Read the nouns under the pictures. Then, write each noun under **One** or **More Than One**.

One   **More Than One**

Homophones

Homophones are words that sound the same but are spelled differently and mean different things.

Write a homophone from the box next to each picture.

so	see	blew	pear

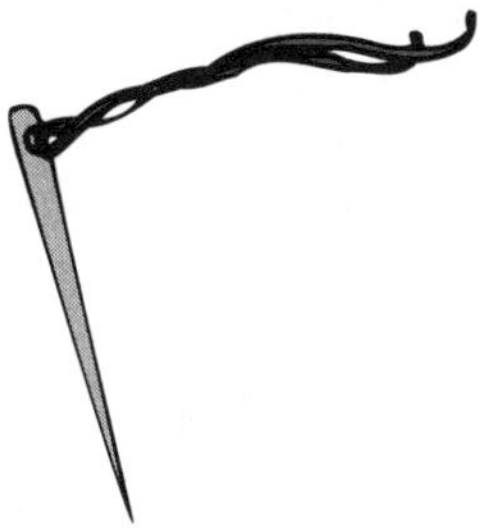

sew _____

pair _____

sea _____

blue _____

Suffixes

A **suffix** is a syllable that is added at the end of a word to change its meaning.

Add the suffixes to the root words to make new words. Use your new words to complete the sentences.

help + ful = _____

care + less = _____

build + er = _____

talk + ed = _____

love + ly = _____

loud + er = _____

1. My mother _____ to my teacher about my homework.

2. The radio was _____ than the television.

3. Sally is always _____ to her mother.

4. A _____ put a new garage on our house.

5. The flowers are _____.

6. It is _____ to cross the street without looking both ways.

Thinking Skills

Read the clues below. Draw an **X** on the houses that do not fit the clues. Circle the correct house.

- The house is white.
- The house has a red door.
- The house has a fence in front of it.

Thinking Skills

Read the clues below. Draw an **X** on the mittens that do not fit the clues. Circle the correct mitten.

- The mitten is green.
- The mitten has 2 different shapes on it.
- The mitten has hearts on it.

Thinking Skills

Read the clues below. Draw an **X** on the numbers that do not fit the clues. Circle the correct number.

- The number is greater than 1.
- The number is less than 6.
- The number is not 2.

7   5

2   0

Thinking Skills

Read the clues below. Draw an **X** on the numbers that do not fit the clues. Circle the correct number.

- The number is less than 7.
- The number is greater than 2.
- The number equals 3 + 1.

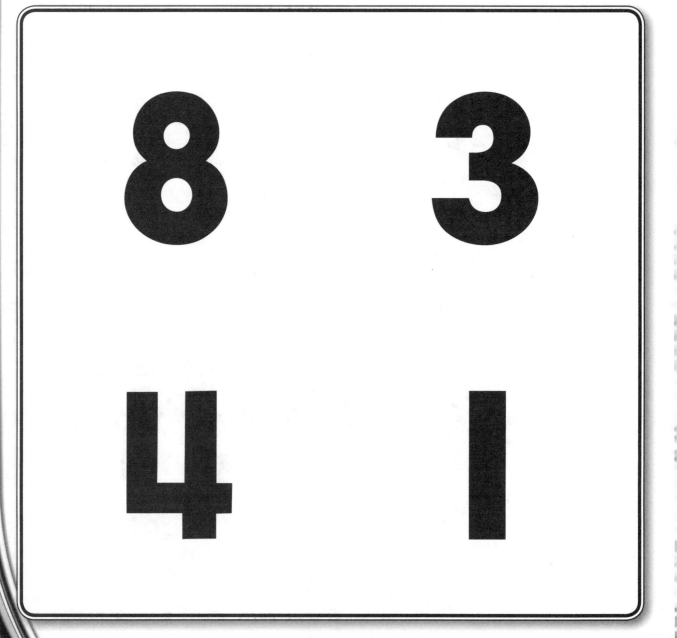

Fourth Quarter Check-Up

Basic Skills

❑ I can sort objects into different categories.

❑ I can put events in time-order.

Reading and Language Arts

❑ I can recognize rhyming words.

❑ I can find antonyms (or opposites) and synonyms.

❑ I can read common, frequently-used words.

❑ I can write sentences that begin with a capital letter and end with a punctuation mark.

❑ I know that a noun is a naming word and a verb is an action word.

❑ I begin names with a capital letter.

❑ I can add **s** to a noun to make it plural.

Math

❑ I can use ordinal numbers **first**, **second**, **third**, etc.

❑ I can count to 100 by ones.

❑ I can count to 100 by tens.

❑ I can add within 10.

❑ I can subtract within 10.

Final Project

Arrange collections, objects found in nature, art projects, and other treasured items to form a museum for friends and family members to visit. Write labels giving each item's name and information about it. Use addition to find the number of items displayed in the museum and include the total on a sign. You may wish to charge a small fee for conducting museum tours.

COMPLETE YEAR KINDERGARTEN

Tt Uu Vv

Ww Xx

Yy Zz

0 1 2 3

4 5 6 7

8 9 10

Colors

Red   Orange   Yellow   Green   Blue   Purple

Brown   Black   White   Gray   Pink

Two-Dimensional Shapes

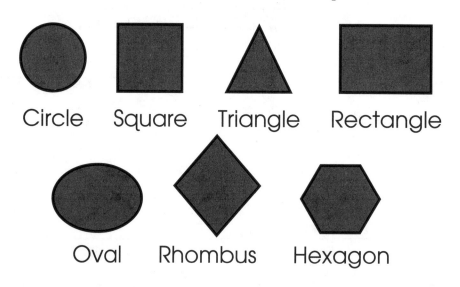

Circle   Square   Triangle   Rectangle

Oval   Rhombus   Hexagon

Three-Dimensional Shapes

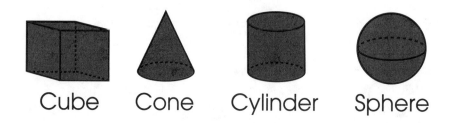

Cube   Cone   Cylinder   Sphere

Numbers 1–100

1	2	3	4	5	6	7	8	9	10
11	12	13	14	15	16	17	18	19	20
21	22	23	24	25	26	27	28	29	30
31	32	33	34	35	36	37	38	39	40
41	42	43	44	45	46	47	48	49	50
51	52	53	54	55	56	57	58	59	60
61	62	63	64	65	66	67	68	69	70
71	72	73	74	75	76	77	78	79	80
81	82	83	84	85	86	87	88	89	90
91	92	93	94	95	96	97	98	99	100

Kindergarten Sight Words

a	for	is	said
at	go	it	see
an	has	like	she
and	have	look	so
am	he	me	the
are	here	my	to
can	in	no	up
do	I	play	we

Recommended Read-Alouds for Kindergarten

- ☐ *Rumble in the Jungle* by Giles Andreae
- ☐ *Cleversticks* by Bernard Ashley
- ☐ *A Handful of Dirt* by Raymond Bial
- ☐ *Friends at School* by Rochelle Bunnett
- ☐ *Ladybug Girl* by Jacky Davis
- ☐ *Kindergarten Rocks!* by Katie Davis
- ☐ *Great Estimations* by Bruce Goldstone
- ☐ *The Three Little Fish and the Big Bad Shark* by Will Grace
- ☐ *Lost and Found* by Oliver Jeffers
- ☐ *Actual Size* by Steve Jenkins
- ☐ *On Earth* by G. Brian Karas
- ☐ *Library Lion* by Michelle Knudsen
- ☐ *Raindrop, Plop* by Wendy Cheyette Lewison
- ☐ *The Opposite* by Tom MacRae
- ☐ *Bee-Bim Bop* by Linda Sue Park
- ☐ *Alphabet Adventure* by Audrey Wood

Answer Key

18

20

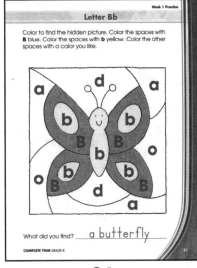

19

21

22

23

Answer Key

24

25

26

28

29

30

Answer Key

31

33

34

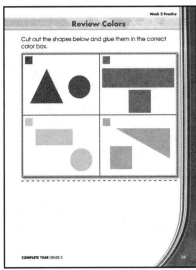

35

38

Answer Key

39

40

41

42

43

44

Answer Key

45

46

48

49

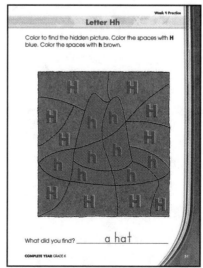

50

51

Answer Key

52

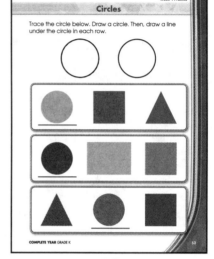

53

54

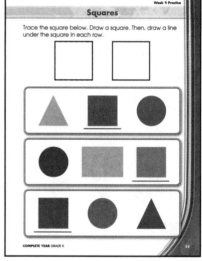

55

56

58

Answer Key

59

60

61

62

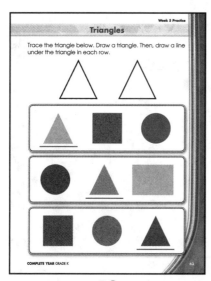

63

64

Answer Key

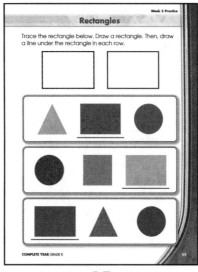

65

66

68

69

70

71

Answer Key

72

74

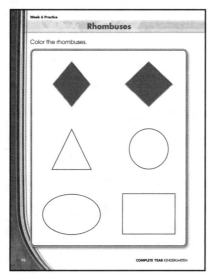

76

73

75

78

Answer Key

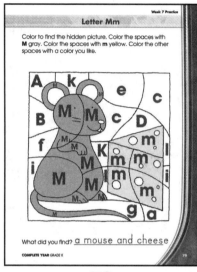

79

80

81

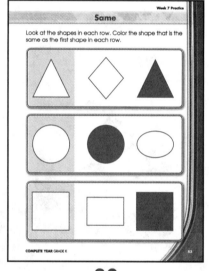

83

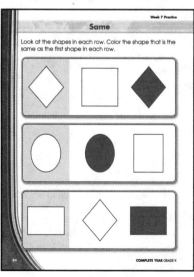

84

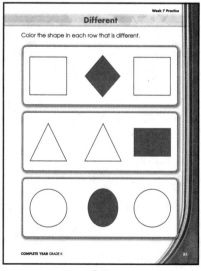

85

Answer Key

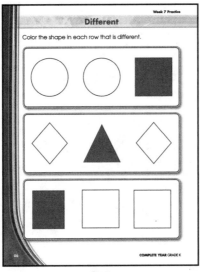

86

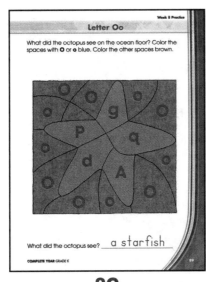

89

91

88

90

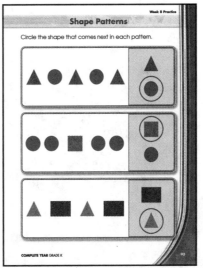

93

Answer Key

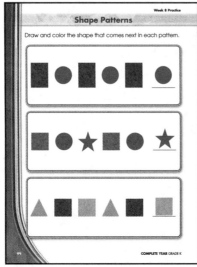

94

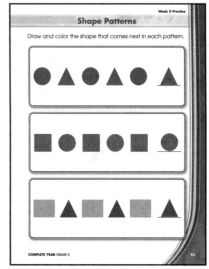

95

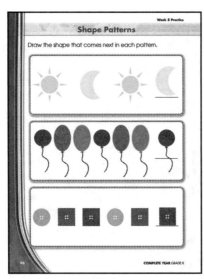

96

98

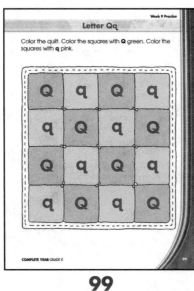

99

100

Answer Key

101

104

103

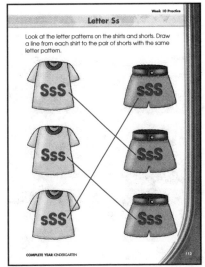

105

112

113

Answer Key

114

115

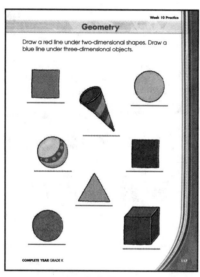

117

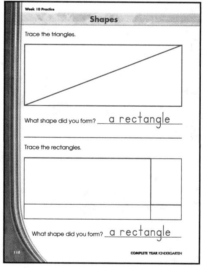

118

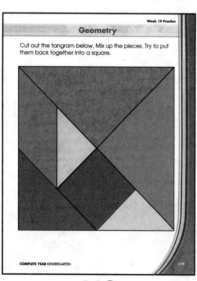

119

122

Answer Key

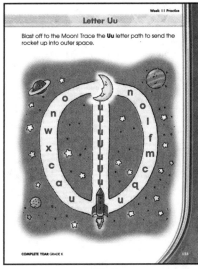

123

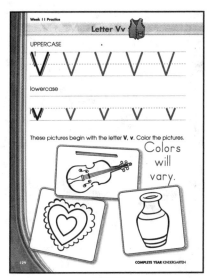

124

125

127

128

129

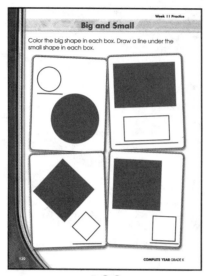

130

132

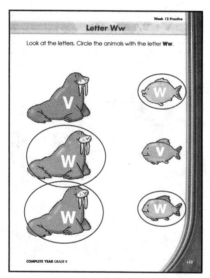

133

134

135

136

Answer Key

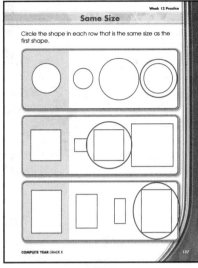

137

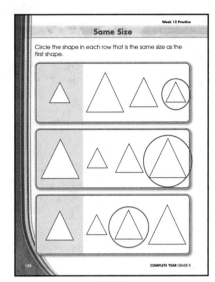

138

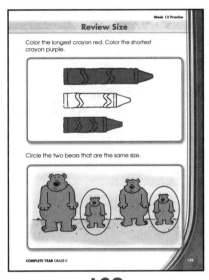

139

140

142

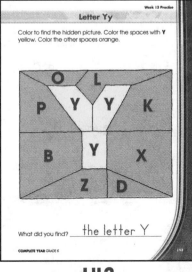

143

Answer Key

144

145

147

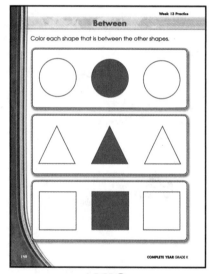

148

149

150

Answer Key

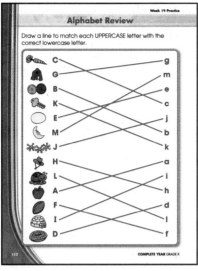

152

153

154

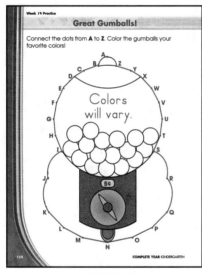

155

156

157

Answer Key

158

159

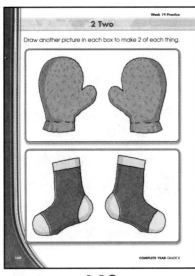

160

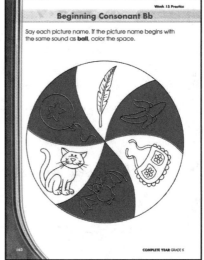

162

163

165

Answer Key

166

167

168

169

170

172

Answer Key

173

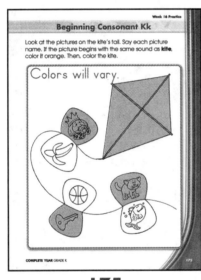

174

175

176

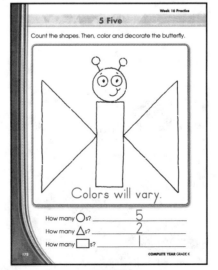

177

178

Answer Key

Week 16 Practice
Review Numbers 1-5
Look at the picture. Read the questions. Circle the correct number.

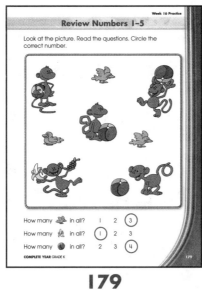

How many 🐒 in all?   1   2   **③**
How many 🐭 in all?   **①**   2   3
How many ⚽ in all?   2   3   **④**

COMPLETE YEAR GRADE K

179

Week 16 Practice
Review Numbers 1-5
Look at the picture. Read the questions. Circle the correct number.

How many 🦋 in all?   **③**   4   5
How many 🐝 in all?   3   **④**   5
How many 🪰 in all?   3   4   **⑤**

COMPLETE YEAR GRADE K

180

Week 17 Practice
Beginning Consonant Mm
Say each picture name. Color the pictures whose names begin with the same sound as **macaroni** and **meatballs**.

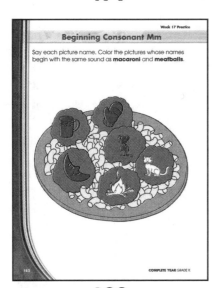

COMPLETE YEAR GRADE K

182

Week 17 Practice
Beginning Consonant Nn
Help the birds find their nest. Follow the path with the pictures whose names begin with the same sound as **nest**.

COMPLETE YEAR GRADE K

183

Week 17 Practice
Beginning Consonant Pp
Pam only packs things whose names begin with the same sound as **panda**. Say the picture names. Circle each picture whose name begins with the same sound as **Pam** and **panda**.

COMPLETE YEAR KINDERGARTEN

184

Week 17 Practice
Beginning Consonant Qq
Look at the pictures on the quilt below. Say each picture name. If the picture begins with the same sound as **quilt**, color the square yellow. Color the other squares purple.

COMPLETE YEAR GRADE K

185

186

187

188

189

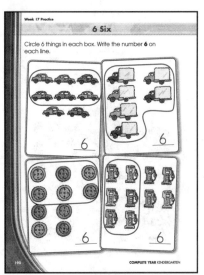

190

192

Answer Key

Beginning Consonant Tt

Say the picture name for each toy in the tub. Draw an **X** on the pictures whose names begin with the same sound as **tub**.

COMPLETE YEAR GRADE K

193

Beginning Consonant Vv

These pictures begin with the letter **Vv**. Color the pictures.

Colors will vary.

BE MINE

valentine

vase

vacuum

violin

COMPLETE YEAR KINDERGARTEN

194

Beginning Consonant Ww

These pictures begin with the letter **Ww**. Color the pictures.

Colors will vary.

wagon

watch

watermelon

window

COMPLETE YEAR KINDERGARTEN

195

Consonant Xx

Write **x** on the lines to complete each picture name. Then, color the big **X**.

exit   x-ray

X

box   fox

COMPLETE YEAR KINDERGARTEN

196

Review Numbers 1–6

Circle the correct number in each box.

3 4 (5)   4 5 (6)

1 (2) 3   2 (3) 4

COMPLETE YEAR GRADE K

197

Review Numbers 1–6

Count each group of blocks. Trace each number. Then, count each group of blocks below. Write the number.

1 2 3 4 5 6

1 2 3 4 5 6

COMPLETE YEAR GRADE K

198

Answer Key

199

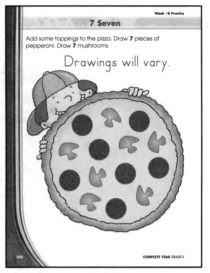

200

206

207

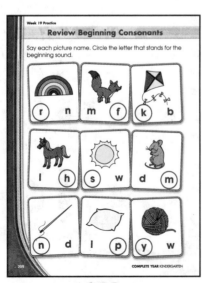

208

209

Answer Key

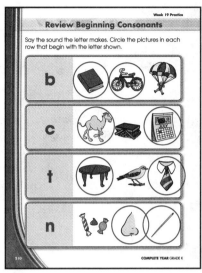

210

211

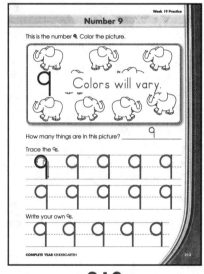

213

214

216

Answer Key

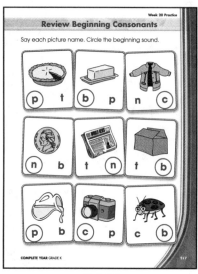

217

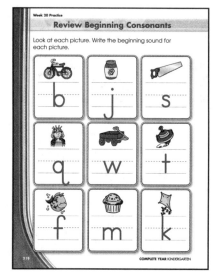

218

219

221

222

223

Answer Key

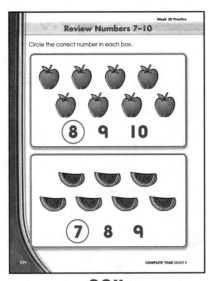

224

226

227

228

229

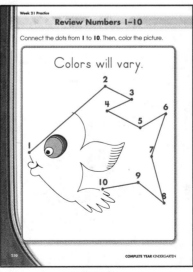

230

Answer Key

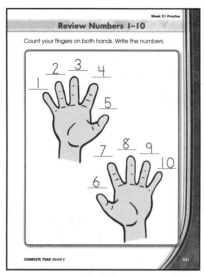

231

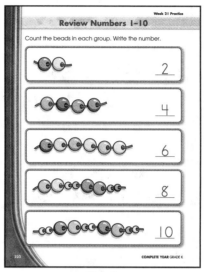

232

233

234

236

237

Answer Key

238

239

240

241

242

243

Answer Key

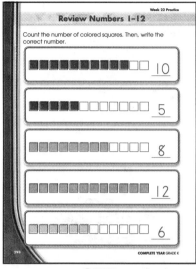

244

246

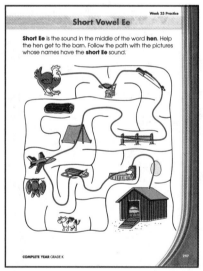

247

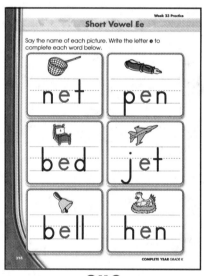

248

249

250

251

252

253

254

256

257

Answer Key

258

259

260

Number 15

This is the number **15**. Color the picture.

Colors will vary.

How many things are in this picture? _15_

Trace the 15s.

Write your own 15s.

261

262

Number 16

This is the number **16**. Color the picture.

Colors will vary.

How many things are in this picture? _16_

Trace the 16s.

Write your own 16s.

263

Answer Key

264

266

267

268

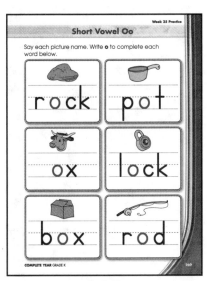

269

270

Answer Key

271

272

273

274

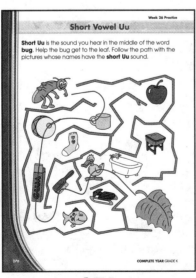

276

277

Answer Key

Week 26 Practice

Short Vowel Uu

Write the letter **u** to complete each word. Read the word. Draw a line to match each word with its picture.

gum

cup

bug

duck

COMPLETE YEAR KINDERGARTEN

279

Week 26 Practice

Short Vowel Uu

Look at the pictures and read the words. Draw a line from each picture to the word that matches it.

cup   bus   gum   mug

COMPLETE YEAR GRADE K

280

Week 26 Practice

Number 19

This is the number **19**. Color the picture.

19

Colors will vary.

How many things are in this picture? _____ 19

Trace the 19s.

19 19 19 19

19 19 19 19

Write your own 19s.

19 19 19 19

COMPLETE YEAR KINDERGARTEN

281

Week 26 Practice

19 Nineteen

Draw **19** cookies in the cookie jar. Color the cookies. Number them from **1** to **19**.

Drawings will vary.

COMPLETE YEAR KINDERGARTEN

282

Week 26 Practice

Number 20

This is the number **20**. Color the picture.

20

Colors will vary.

How many things are in this picture? _____ 20

Trace the 20s.

20 20 20

20 20 20

Write your own 20s.

20 20 20

COMPLETE YEAR KINDERGARTEN

283

Week 26 Practice

20 Twenty

Draw **20** freckles on the boy's face. Color the boy.

Colors will vary.

COMPLETE YEAR KINDERGARTEN

284

Answer Key

286

287

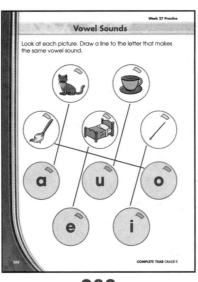

288

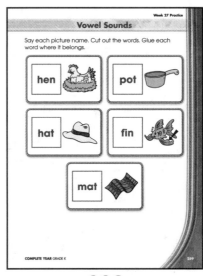

289

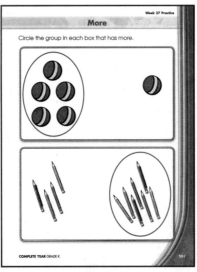

291

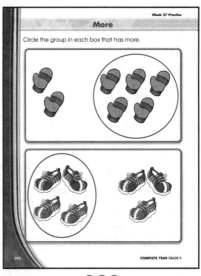

292

Answer Key

293

294

300

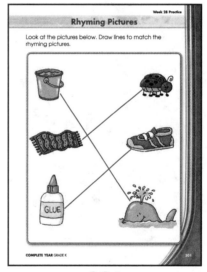

301

302

303

Answer Key

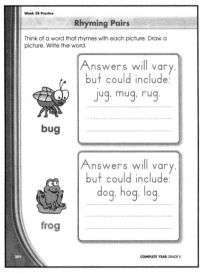

304

305

306

307

308

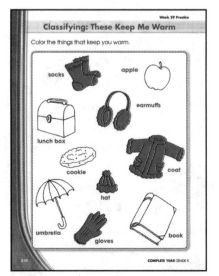

310

Answer Key

311

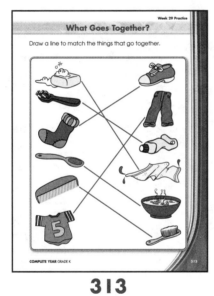

312

313

314

315

316

Answer Key

317

318

320

321

322

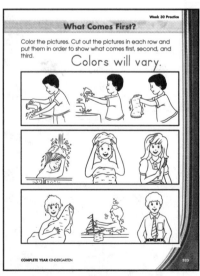

323

Answer Key

325

326

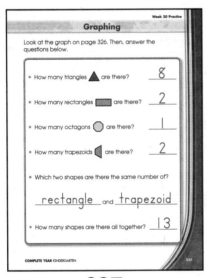

327

328

330

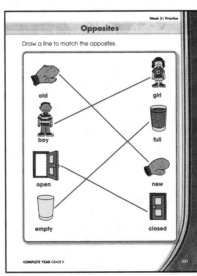

331

Answer Key

332

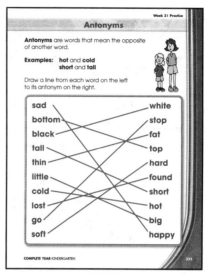

333

334

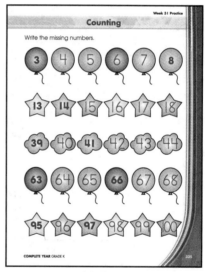

335

336

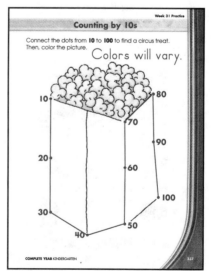

337

Answer Key

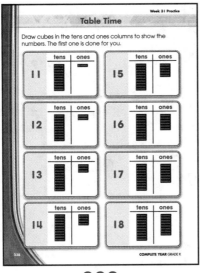

338

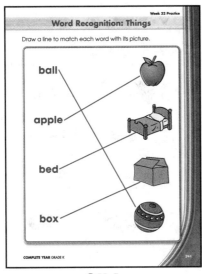

341

342

343

344

Answer Key

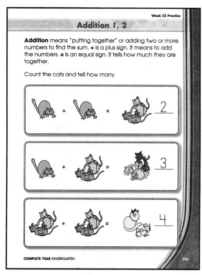

345

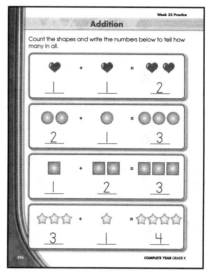

346

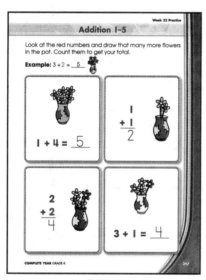

347

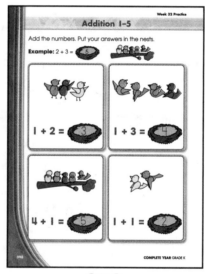

348

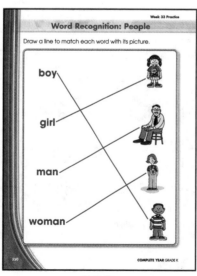

350

351

Answer Key

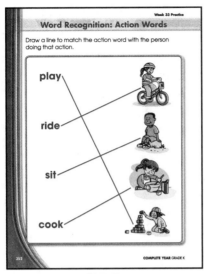

352

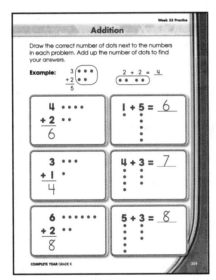

353

355

356

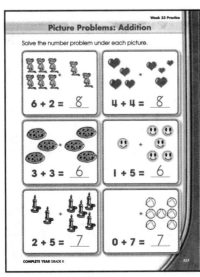

357

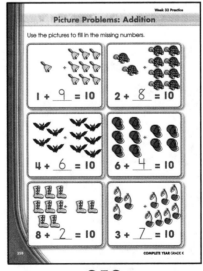

358

Answer Key

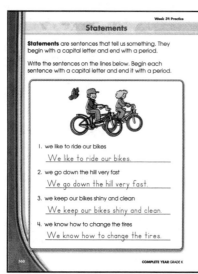

360

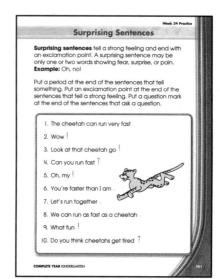

361

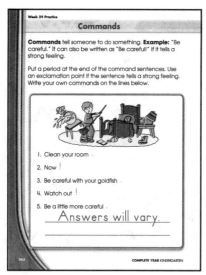

362

363

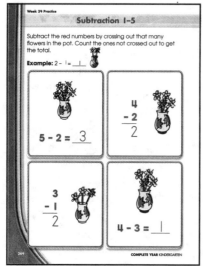

364

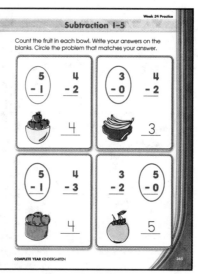

365

Answer Key

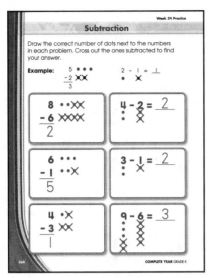

366

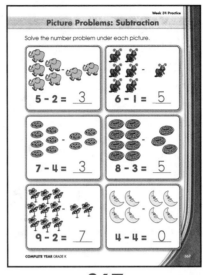

367

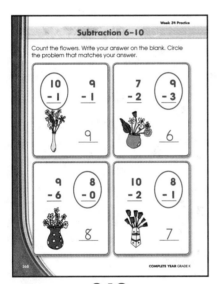

368

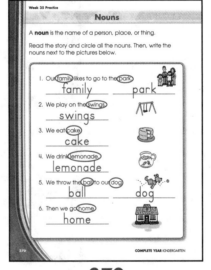

370

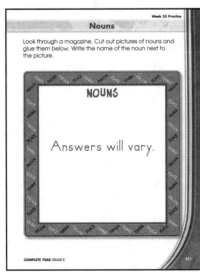

371

372

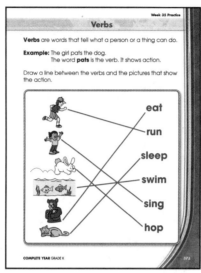

373

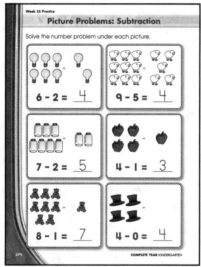

374

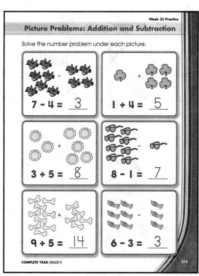

375

Answer Key

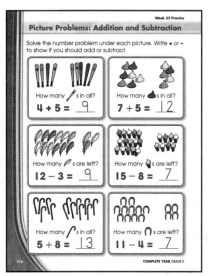

376

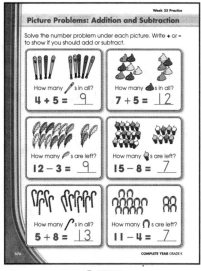

377

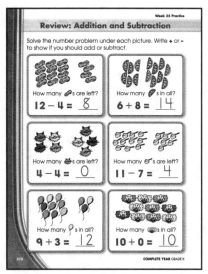

378

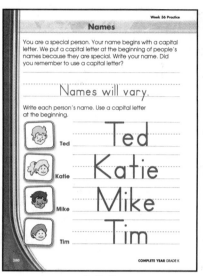

380

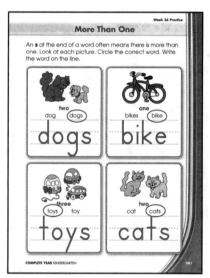

381

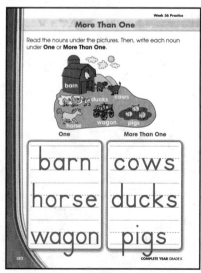

382

Answer Key

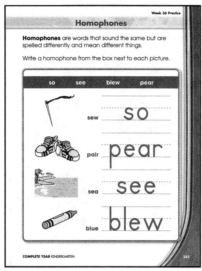

383

384

385

Answer Key

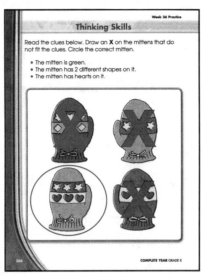

386

387

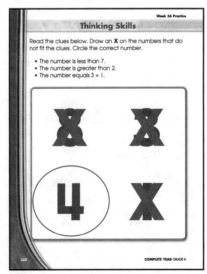

388